AUTOCAD LT 2000

in easy steps

Paul Whelan

COMPUTER
STEP

In easy steps is an imprint of Computer Step
Southfield Road. Southam
Warwickshire CV47 OFB. England

Tel: 01926 817999 Fax: 01926 817005
http://www.computerstep.com

Notice of Liability

Trademarks

Printed and bound in the United Kingdom

ISBN 1-84078-101-7

Contents

5   How to Edit Objects   55

6   Text, Points and Units   71

7   Working with Layers   83

8   Blocks and Xrefs   99

9   Dimensioning   125

Fundamental Concepts

In this chapter, you'll learn the difference between traditional draughting techniques and those used in AutoCAD LT 2000. You will then start AutoCAD LT and become familiar with the Create New Drawing dialog box. Setting the drawing units and the electronic paper size are concepts that must be understood before you draw; these are covered in detail. The layout of the AutoCAD LT screen is then described in conjunction with the different methods of giving the program commands. Lastly, emphasis is placed on the importance of the command line.

Covers

Chapter One

Traditional Draughting Techniques

Let us take a look at how you might set about drawing in the traditional way on paper. Before starting to draw, you decide on:

A scale of 1:1 means one unit on your drawing is the same as one unit in reality.

Scale

A drawing of an object that in reality is larger than your sheet of paper (such as an extension to a house) must be scaled down. Something that is too small to represent comfortably on paper (such as the face of a watch) must be scaled up.

Paper size

You must select the size of paper on which the drawing will fit: eg, A4, A3, A2, etc.

It's useful to know the size of sheets:

A4 = 297mm X 210mm
A3 = 420mm X 297mm
A2 = 594mm X 420mm
A1 = 841mm X 594mm
A0 = 1189mm X 841mm.

Units

The units you use depend on the conventions expected by the engineers, designers, or builders. You may for example work in the imperial or metric systems. Values may be so small that you have to use 'scientific' or exponential notation to dimension a drawing.

Drawing instruments

Drawing tools such as a T-square, pens, erasers and ruler must be close at hand. Precision drawing tools are expensive and need to be maintained and replaced.

Drawing-board

A good board is essential to aid you in the accurate execution of the drawing.

Much time is spent trying to draw accurately with a pen. AutoCAD LT 2000 takes care of most of this for you if you learn to use the tools.

The drawing process

During a draughtperson's traditional training they learn to draw accurately the basic elements of a drawing: lines, arcs, circles, etc. Much time is spent selecting points accurately: the beginning and end points of lines, arcs, etc, and calculating distances.

Construction lines need to be drawn to locate points. Eventually, many of these construction lines will be erased.

AutoCAD LT Draughting Techniques

 AutoCAD LT 2000 works in Real Size scale (1=1).

Scale

The problem of scaling is solved in a very dramatic way: there is NO scaling while producing your drawing in AutoCAD LT 2000. All the dimensions you enter are input in real size (1=1). AutoCAD LT 2000 refers to this as inputting your drawing in Real World Co-ordinates. The computer magnifys the image to display it on the screen.

Paper size

When your drawing is completed, you decide on the scale you want it printed on paper. A paper size is then selected which can accommodate the drawing.

 If a table is 130cm by 75cm, you draw it 130*75cm in AutoCAD LT 2000. Similarly, if a watch part has a 0.125mm diameter in reality, it is drawn 0.125 of a millimetre.

Electronic paper size

While working in AutoCAD LT 2000 you draw in real world size, 1=1. This means that you must set up an electronic sheet of paper on the computer big enough to hold the drawing at 1=1.

For example, to set up an area on the computer screen to draw a ship of dimensions 210 metres by 32 metres you must tell AutoCAD LT 2000 that you need an electronic sheet at least 210 by 32 metres. You would probably set up a sheet of 250 by 50 metres. This will be enough space to accommodate the ship.

Units

This command allows you to set up the units you wish to work with.

Drawing instruments

AutoCAD LT 2000 provides 'tools' to help you draw accurately. For example, you can snap onto existing lines or circles.

 If you want to draw a building, then the electronic sheet of paper must be a bit bigger than the building!

Drawing board

This instrument has obviously been dispensed with.

The drawing process

AutoCAD LT 2000 drawings are constructed from pre-defined objects such as lines, arcs and circles. There is a command for each object type (Line, Circle, etc.).

Starting and Finishing AutoCAD LT

There is a difference between 'Cancel' and 'OK' on the dialog boxes: OK keeps the changes you made in the box; 'Cancel' does not.

Starting AutoCAD LT 2000 on Windows 95/98/NT and 2000

Click on the AutoCAD LT 2000 icon on the desktop. If no icon is present, click on 'Start' on the taskbar.

Next, move the pointer to 'Programs'. Then move the pointer to the AutoCAD LT 2000 folder and click on the AutoCAD LT 2000 icon.

Dialog boxes

AutoCAD LT will display many dialog boxes while you work. These dialog boxes:

- Show the current settings.

- Allow you to change some settings if you wish.

The 'OK', 'Cancel', 'Close' and 'Done' buttons

If a dialog box appears that you do not want, click the 'Cancel' button. You can also press the Esc button at the top left of the keyboard.

If you change any settings in a dialog box and you want AutoCAD LT 2000 to use the new settings then click on 'OK'.

'Done' is similar to 'OK'. Click on 'Done' when you have completed modifying the dialog box.

'Close' will appear on some dialog boxes. This is similar to 'Cancel'.

You may select the top right button icon 'X' to close the dialog box without saving any changes.

If you do not save your work before you finish the program, it may ask you to 'Save changes to drawing'. The option Cancel will cancel the command to exit from AutoCAD LT 2000.

Finishing AutoCAD LT 2000

Save your drawing and then click on the 'x' button or under the File menu: File > Exit.

'Create New Drawing' Dialog Box

This dialog box sets up the electronic sheet size and the units for drawing. The AutoCAD LT 2000 dialog box is shown here. The AutoCAD 95, 97 and 98 dialog boxes are similar. Users of LT previous to the 95 release have a different dialog box – see page 14.

Opens an existing drawing

Use this to start a drawing. You need more than a beginners knowledge to use this option

Use an existing template

If you do not have the 'Startup' dialog box on screen, select 'File' from the menu and click on 'New'.

Tells you what each of the above buttons does

Contents change according to the button you select

Try clicking on each of the buttons to see the changes in the dialog box.

What is a Wizard?

A 'Wizard' helps you to carry out a task which you may not have had time to learn. Two Wizards are available: Quick Setup and Advanced Setup.

Click on 'Use a Wizard'

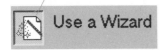

Click on the 'Use a Wizard' button if it is not already selected and then select the 'Quick Setup' Wizard from the list by highlighting it.

Click on 'OK' to start the Wizard.

The Drawing Units

The Wizard proceeds to the 'Quick Setup' dialog box. This dialog box has two tabs: one for setting up the drawing units and the other to set the size of the electronic page or drawing area.

Step 1: Units

AutoCAD LT wants to know which units you want to use while drawing. There are five fundamental types of units. Click on each of the units to see a sample.

I unit = Imm

Decimal refers to millimetres (mm).

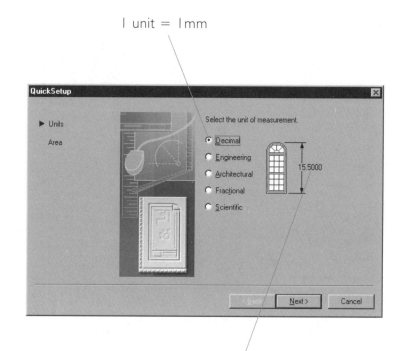

If you decide not to proceed with the setup, you must click 'Cancel'.

The number of decimal places can be set using the Units dialog box later

The units selected here are used by AutoCAD LT 2000 for dimensioning the drawing. Also, input from the user is accepted in these units only.

To proceed, select 'Decimal' and then click the 'Next' button to set the Area.

The Electronic Paper Size

You cannot ignore a dialog box. It demands a response from you. Clicking on any other part of the computer screen will not banish it. You must click 'Done' or 'Cancel'.

The size of the electronic sheet of paper must be large enough to contain the drawing in real size (1=1). If you are going to plot the finished drawing on standard paper sizes (A3, A2, A1, etc.), keep the proportions of the electronic sheet as a multiple of the standard paper sizes.

An example

Imagine the building you must draw is 30 by 20 metres. Convert this to mm by multiplying by 1000 (because you selected decimal (mm) as your unit in 'Step 1'). This is 30*1000 = 30,000mm; 20*1000 = 20,000mm. This building will fit on an A3 (420mm*297mm) sheet multiplied by 100 – ie, (420mm*297mm)*100 = 42,000*29,700.

This is the electronic sheet size you want. It will hold the building in real size (1=1). You can later plot the work onto an A3 sheet by reducing the drawing by a factor of 100 (ie, plot at 1=100).

Step 2: Area

To tell AutoCAD LT 2000 that this is the electronic sheet size you want, enter 42,000 by 29,700 in the dialog box (do not type in the thousand separator comma mark).

1   Double-click here. When the text is highlighted in blue, proceed to type in the electronic page size.

2   Type 42000.

3   Type 29700.

4   Click 'Finish'.

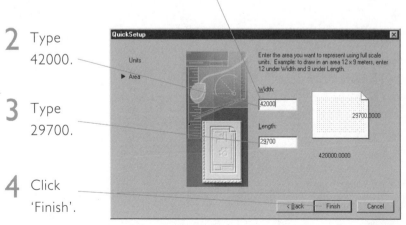

AutoCAD LT Release 2 Setup

The 'Create New Drawing' dialog box for releases of AutoCAD LT previous to the 95, 97 and 98 editions is visually different, but it requires the same information: the drawing units and the electronic page size.

If you do not have the 'Create New Drawing' dialog box displayed on the screen, select 'File' from the menu and click 'New'.

1 Click here to select the 'Quick' method.

2 Make sure you have a tick here if you want this dialog box to appear when you start AutoCAD LT the next time.

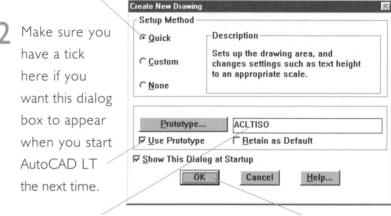

3 The prototype offered should be the *acltiso* file for the metric system.

4 Click OK.

5 Choose *Decimal* here. Click the down-arrow to see the range of available units.

Leave the 'Turn On Snap' box blank for now. Later, you can turn this command on simply by clicking the box to place a tick in it.

6 Type 42000 and 29700 – see page 13 on how to calculate these values.

7 (Optional) Tick here to display a grid on the drawing to show the size of the electronic sheet.

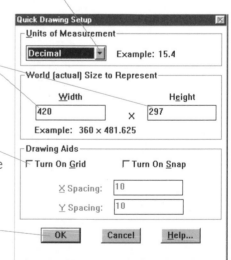

8 Click 'OK' to proceed.

AutoCAD LT's Drawing Screen

Object
Properties
toolbar

Pull-down menus
contain the drawing &
editing commands

Standard toolbar with
frequently used
commands displayed

**AutoCAD
LT releases
previous
to LT
2000 may have
different screens,
but most of the
elements are still
present.**

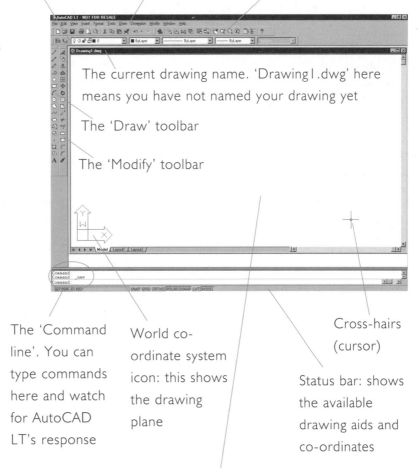

The current drawing name. 'Drawing1.dwg' here
means you have not named your drawing yet

The 'Draw' toolbar

The 'Modify' toolbar

The 'Command
line'. You can
type commands
here and watch
for AutoCAD
LT's response

World co-
ordinate system
icon: this shows
the drawing
plane

Cross-hairs
(cursor)

Status bar: shows
the available
drawing aids and
co-ordinates

The drawing editor: this is where you draw. The grid of
dots shows the size of the electronic sheet you set up

Just below the World co-ordinate system icon are three
tabs: Model, Layout1 and Layout2. Model is highlighted
showing that your view of the screen is Model Space. This
is where the drawing is constructed. The Layout1/2 refer to
Paper Space which is used to print the drawing.

Giving Commands to AutoCAD LT

Pull-down menus

Just click on the menu name to see the list of commands. Click on a command to issue it. If a command has an arrow after it, a sub-menu appears when you move the arrow cursor over it. Click on a command in the sub-menu to issue it. If a command has three omission points after it (...) a dialog box appears when the command is selected.

If you use a short-cut you do not need to pull down a menu. Ctrl+S saves the drawing.

Omission points lead to a dialog box

Arrow leads to a sub-menu

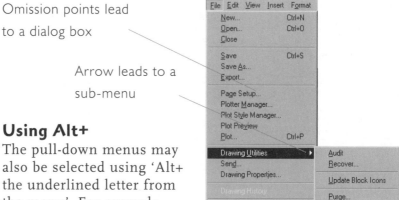

Using Alt+

The pull-down menus may also be selected using 'Alt+ the underlined letter from the menu'. For example, hold down the Alt key and press the 'F' key to pull down the File menu.

Shortcuts

For example, Ctrl+S issues the Save command even if the pull-down menu is not activated.

Right-clicking

Shortcut menus appear when you right-click the mouse (or other pointing device). The shortcut menu changes as you right-click on different areas of the screen.

Try right-clicking over the drawing editor and then over the standard toolbar to see this 'context sensitive' option in action.

A menu displayed as a result of a right-click of the mouse with the cursor over the drawing editor

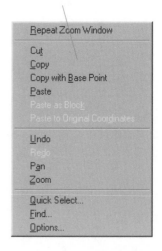

...cont'd

Toolbars can be dragged out on to the drawing editor where they become floating toolbars. These floating toolbars can be moved around the screen.

Toolbar

Many commands can be issued by just clicking the appropriate icon from the toolbars.

Cursor menu

These menus are called up using the Shift key and a mouse button other than the 'click' (or left-mouse) button:

If you have a two-button mouse hold down Shift and right-click.

If you have a three-button mouse or an Intellimouse use Shift and the middle button or wheel.

The Command line

The command line at the bottom of the drawing editor is very important when drawing with AutoCAD LT. You must keep checking what is written here as you draw and edit.

For example, if you draw a line AutoCAD LT needs to know where the line starts and ends. It asks for these locations on the command line.

Again if you want to erase a line or a circle, AutoCAD LT asks you to choose which line or circle to delete, at the command line. The importance of the command line cannot be overemphasized.

Here are two examples of the command line requesting input from the user:

AutoCAD LT needs to know where the line starts and ends

```
Command: 1
LINE From point:
To point:
0.8709< 25                    SNAP GRID ORTHO OSNAP MODEL TILE
```

Here AutoCAD LT requests the location of the centre point of the circle and its radius

```
Command: c
CIRCLE 3P/2P/TTR/<Center point>: Diameter/<Radius>:
Command:
-2.5886,1.1716               SNAP GRID ORTHO OSNAP MODEL TILE
```

You must keep your eye on the command line when drawing and editing. AutoCAD LT 'talks' to you there.

Saving a Drawing for the First Time

You could call up the 'Save As' dialog box with the keystrokes Alt+F and then A. That is, hold down the Alt key and press F. This will 'drop-down' the menu. Then press A for the underlined letter in 'Save As'.

A drawing that has no name is entitled **[Drawing]**. You should give the drawing a name as soon as you set it up. Don't wait until you have drawn some objects. All the settings such as the size of the drawing sheet and the units used are saved as part of the file.

Save and Save As

You can save a drawing in two ways. Both are found on the File menu. One is to use the 'Save' command, the other method uses the 'Save As' command.

Generally, use 'Save As' if (1) you're saving a drawing for the first time (as in this case) and (2) if the drawing already has a name (other than 'Drawing') and you want to rename it as something else. Use 'Save' if the drawing is named.

1 Click on the drop-down menu 'File'.

2 Click on 'Save As'. The 'Save Drawing As' dialog appears.

3 Type in a file name and click on 'Save'.

The drawing is saved into the folder that is open here

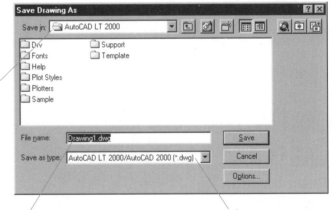

Windows uses full stops for filename extensions.

Type the file name you want here – up to 32 characters long. Do not use a full stop

This shows you the type of drawing file you're saving

Basic Drawing Techniques

In this chapter, you'll learn the basic drawing techniques employed by AutoCAD LT 2000. Great emphasis is placed on reading what is displayed at the command line. Recovering from errors in both your use of AutoCAD LT 2000 and in creating a drawing is outlined. The commands for drawing a circle and moving an entity are examined in detail. Mastering these commands is essential if you want to make progress in understanding what AutoCAD LT 2000 expects from you, the user. As a further aid to drawing accurately, we examine snapping to an object using the end point of a line and the centre of a circle as examples. Finally, you learn how to switch these Object Snap options on as background tools.

Covers

Chapter Two

Drawing a Line

The Command **LINE** (or simply **L** typed at the Command line) draws line entities in the drawing editor.

Use the keyboard short-cut, Ctrl+S to save your drawing regularly.

How the Command works

When the command is executed, AutoCAD LT 2000 asks you to specify the start and end points of the line. Remember, you can use the Command line, the drop-down menu or the toolbar.

Regardless of the method you use to give the command, you must look down at the Command line to see how AutoCAD LT is responding.

Instead of pressing Enter you could just press the Spacebar.

Use one of these methods:

- At the Command line just type L and press Enter

- On the drop-down menu 'Draw,' click on Line, or

- On the toolbar click on the line icon

AutoCAD LT asks: 'LINE Specify firstpoint:'. Pick a point and move the mouse. AutoCAD LT now asks you to 'Specify next point or [Undo]:'. Pick another point. AutoCAD LT 2000 asks 'Specify next point' until you press Enter.

Click on the first point in response to 'Specify firstpoint'

Monitor the command line when you issue commands.

AutoCAD LT 2000 keeps asking 'Specify next point or [Undo]' until you press Enter to terminate the command

What to do if you Make a Mistake

Press Esc to cancel a command. When the command line is blank, it is ready to accept another command. Users of AutoCAD Release 2 need to press Ctrl+C to cancel.

Two types of mistake frequently occur: mistakes associated with using AutoCAD LT 2000 itself and mistakes in the actual drawing you are currently working on.

Pressing the Esc key

The Esc key at the top left of the keyboard solves most problems you may meet in AutoCAD LT 2000. Here are some examples when you might press the Esc key. When:

- a command does not respond the way you expect
- you want to cancel a command
- you click a point on the screen unintentionally
- a dialog box appears on the screen accidentally

In all the above examples, pressing Esc once frees the command line. When the command line is blank you can proceed to issue a new command. In some cases you may need to press the Esc key twice. For example, if you are dimensioning an entity and you decide you would like to return to a blank command line.

You may need to press Esc twice to cancel out of dimensioning, or if little blue boxes called Grips appear in the drawing.

Using Undo

You can undo the last command by typing U at the command line and pressing the Enter key, or by clicking on the Undo icon on the toolbar. You may undo several commands by clicking on the down-arrow beside the Undo icon and selecting the actions you want undone by highlighting them.

All releases of AutoCAD LT previous to LT 98 allowed you to only redo the last command you applied Undo to.

Using Redo

The Redo command reinstates the last command you apply Undo to. You may Redo several commands which were undone by clicking on the down-arrow beside the Redo icon and selecting the actions you want to Redo by highlighting them.

Drawing a Circle

The Circle command ends on its own, whereas the Line command continues until you press Enter to terminate it.

To draw a circle, choose one of the following options:

Command line: circle, or the alias 'c'

Menu: Draw > Circle

Toolbar:

How the command works

When the Circle command is issued AutoCAD LT needs to know where the centre of the circle is to be and its radius or diameter. The command line prompts: 'CIRCLE Specify center point for circle or [3P/2P/Ttr (tan tan radius)]:'. If you click a point on the screen, AutoCAD LT accepts that point as the centre of the circle. If you don't want to click the centre of the circle and instead use a different option, you must type the capitalised letter(s) of the option required. To draw a circle through three specified points type 3P at the command line and press the Enter key. TTR must be typed to draw a circle with a radius that is a tangent to two objects.

The <angled brackets> show the option that AutoCAD LT is offering you.

Drawing with the Circle default options

In response to: 'CIRCLE Specify center point for circle or [3P/2P/Ttr (tan tan radius)]:' click a point on the screen. The command line displays: 'Specify radius of circle or [Diameter]'. Radius is the default option. If you move the mouse, a circle forms specified by the size of the radius you are showing AutoCAD LT. Pick a point. AutoCAD LT 2000 draws a circle and the command line is left blank.

To select an option other than the default, you must type in the capitalised letter(s) offered at the command prompt.

AutoCAD LT allows you to draw a circle by specifying the endpoints of a diameter.

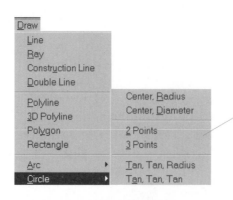

Various options for drawing a circle are available on this sub-menu

Moving an Entity

 To tell AutoCAD LT 2000 you have finished selecting objects, just press the Enter key.

To move any entity, choose one of the following options:

Command line: move, or the alias 'm'

Menu: Modify > Move

Toolbar:

How the command works

AutoCAD LT 2000 needs to know which object you want to move. This requires that you select the object or objects. You then need to specify where you want to pick up the object and where you want to place it. If you wish you can give the distance you want to displace or move the object.

 If you miss the object you are trying to select, a box appears at the cursor. Just move the box so it crosses over the entity and click again.

Using the Move command

Issue the Move command. The command line displays 'Select objects:' and the cursor changes to a pickbox. Place the pickbox over the circle's perimeter and click once. The circle is highlighted if you succeed. The prompt shows: 'Select objects: 1 found', Select objects:'. At this point, press Enter to tell AutoCAD LT that you have finished selecting objects. The command line changes to 'Specify base point or displacement:'. AutoCAD LT wants to know where you will pick up the object. Click anywhere near or on the circle. The command line displays 'Specify second point of displacement or <use first point as displacement>'. Now you can move the circle by moving the mouse and pick the location to position the circle. The command terminates itself and gives you a blank command line.

 If the pickbox is too small, just type 'pickbox' at the command line and increase its value. The default size is 3.

 You can use polar co-ordinates to move an object an exact distance.

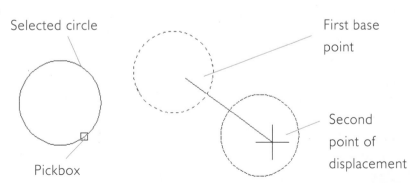

Selected circle

Pickbox

First base point

Second point of displacement

Using Grid and Snap

 The F7 key toggles the grid on/off.

 The size of the grid may be changed at any time by typing GRID at the command line and entering a new value.

 The F9 key toggles the snap on/off.

 If you draw outside the grid area, you are drawing outside the electronic page you set up.

 If the grid setting is too small, AutoCAD LT will refuse to display it.

The Grid

The grid is an array of dots placed over the drawing. It is a drawing aid and does not print – it is not part of the drawing. A grid has three main functions: it shows the size of the electronic sheet you set up; you can snap the cross-hairs to the grid; when you magnify the drawing with the Zoom command the distance between the grid points will give you an idea of how much you have magnified the image. The grid can be switched on/off at any time using the status line by a single pick on the GRID button.

Snap

When Snap is not active, the cross-hairs move smoothly across the drawing editor. Snap causes the cross-hairs to move in jumps. For example, setting the Snap to 25mm allows you to quickly draw lines of 25mm or multiples thereof. You will not be able to draw between the 25mm setting unless you switch snap off. Often the Snap and Grid settings are the same (say 25mm) but they do not have to be equal. Snap can be switched on/off from the status line.

Snap is useful for doing a quick sketch with straight edges.

You can also use a special Snap to lock on to the elements you have already drawn. See Object Snap on page 26.

Ortho

Ortho mode allows you to draw lines either vertically or horizontally. The F8 key toggles the ortho mode on and off. You can also single-click on ORTHO on the status line.

The Ortho mode is the equivalent of using a T-square in traditional draughting.

Switches Snap, Grid and Ortho modes on/off with a single-click

Drawing Aids

If you do not keep your eye on the command line you will not be able to use AutoCAD LT 2000.

AutoCAD LT 2000 has several drawing aids. These are available through the menu sequence: Tools > Drafting Settings. The dialog box has three tabs.

The Isometric Snap area within the dialog box is only used for isometric drawing. It sets up three isoplanes. In this mode, a circle will appear elliptical.

It's a good idea to look at this dialog box before you start working. All the settings can be changed at any time during the drawing procedure. The most important aids are the grid and snap settings.

Switches the Snap on/off

Sets the snap size

Switches the Grid on/off

Sets the size of the grid in the current drawing units

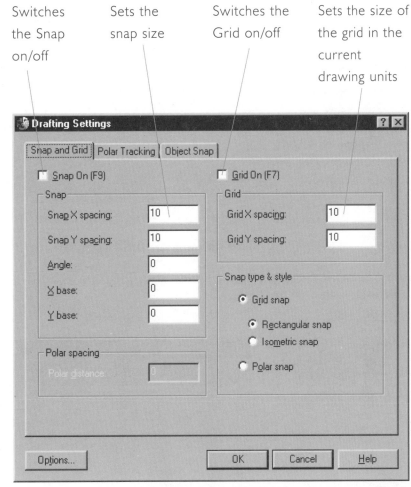

Typing ddrmodes at the command lines displays the Drafting Settings dialog box.

Snapping to Objects – the Toolbar

A toolbar can be dragged to any location on the screen and resized.

By their nature CAD drawings have to be accurate. Joining drawing objects such as lines, arcs and circles should never be done just using your eye. AutoCAD LT has many tools to allow you to lock on to the end of a line or the centre of a circle. These are known as the Object Snap tools and are found on the Object Snap toolbar.

To display the Object Snap Toolbar

Use the menu command sequence: View > Toolbars... The following dialog box displays:

The Toolbars dialog box can be called up by moving the cursor over any existing toolbar and right-clicking.

The tick displays the toolbar

Click once to place/remove the tick

List of available toolbars

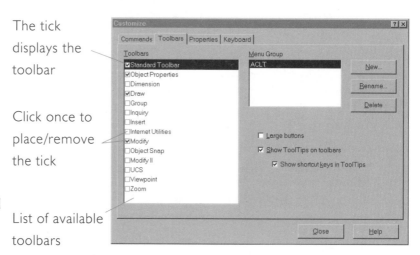

The Object Snap Toolbar

Do not use snap and Object Snap at the same time.

Tracking   Intersection   Perpendicular   None

Endpoint   Quadrant   Node

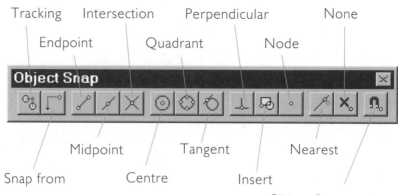

Snap from   Midpoint   Centre   Tangent   Insert   Nearest

Object Snap settings

Snapping to Objects – an Example

Display the Object Snap toolbar (see page 26). Draw a line and a circle near each other on the screen. Now move the circle using Object Snap to the end of the line so that the centre of the circle is located exactly on the end of the line, as follows:

If you fail to read what is displayed at the command line, you will not be able to draw with accuracy.

1 Issue the Move command and read the command line.

2 Pick the circle in response to 'select objects'.

Always use the Object Snap to ensure accuracy.

3 Press Enter to tell AutoCAD LT that there is nothing else you want to select.

4 In response to 'Specify base point or displacement' click on 'Snap to Center' from the Object Snap toolbar. The command line now displays 'cen of' (meaning centre of?).

Try typing some of the commands instead of clicking on them from menus, to help make you more command-line aware.

5 Move the mouse down to the periphery of the selected circle. When a small red selection circle appears at the centre of the selected circle, click the left mouse button.

6 AutoCAD LT picks up the circle at its centre point and the command line displays: 'Specify second point of displacement:'.

7 Click on 'Snap to Endpoint' from the Object Snap toolbar and move the cursor down over the line towards the end at which you want to place the circle. The command line displays 'endp of'.

Never try to join objects by relying on your eye. Always use snap to objects.

8 A red selection box appears towards one end of the line. Click when you see this. The circle then locks into position.

Running Object Snap Tools

If you find the cursor behaving in a way you don't understand, try switching Object Snap off. It's easy to forget when you may have it 'On'.

If you perform a lot of editing, you may find that you are constantly selecting from the Object Snap toolbar. You can overcome this repetition by setting up a running Object Snap.

This feature allows you to preset and switch on the Object Snaps you frequently use. When the running Object Snap is switched on, the cursor automatically selects those 'snaps' as soon as you approach an entity.

Setting up Object Snap

Command line: osnap, or the alias 'os'

Menu: Tools > Drafting Settings, and pick the
                   Object Snap tab

Status Bar: Single-click on OSNAP at the bottom of
                   the screen to toggle the setting on/off

                   Or press the F3 key.

Object
Snap tab

A tick mark
here, shows
Object Snap
is turned on
(active)

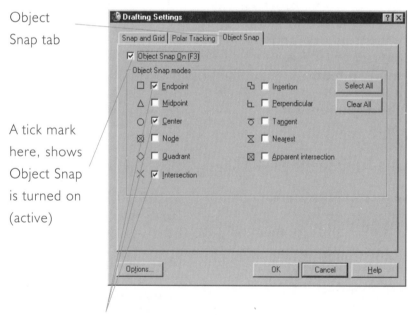

Once the running Object Snap is set up, it can be toggled on/off by a single click on OSNAP on the status line.

Click the boxes to place a tick mark
in the Object Snaps you want to use

Accuracy and Speed

In this chapter, you'll learn how to speed up drawing and editing by using some of AutoCAD LT 2000's sophisticated tools. Aliases, Aerial views and snapping to objects increase speed and accuracy dramatically. It is worth concentrating on these until they are mastered. Using co-ordinate input is essential for any work that requires specific dimensions. You may think you can survive without Grips – until you know how to use them! They save time and ensure accuracy.

Covers

Chapter Three

Opening an Existing Drawing

Command line: open

Menu: File > Open

Double-clicking on a filename automatically opens it into AutoCAD LT 2000.

Toolbar:

AutoCAD LT 2000 allows you to have several drawings open at the same time. Each drawing is opened into its own window. The Select File dialog box is shown below.

This is the current (active) folder

Cick here if you want to look on the desktop

This a preview image of the highlighted drawing

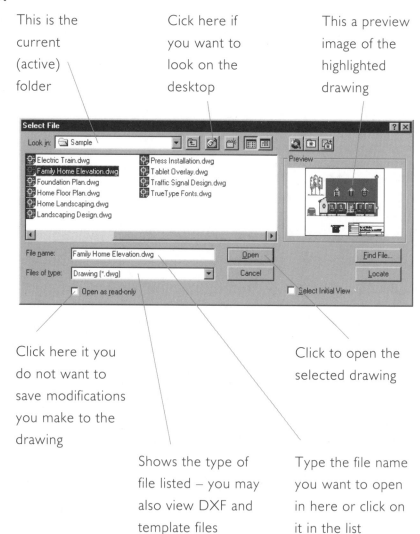

Click here it you do not want to save modifications you make to the drawing

Shows the type of file listed – you may also view DXF and template files

Type the file name you want to open in here or click on it in the list

Click to open the selected drawing

Using Co-ordinate Input

You cannot type a space when inputting the co-ordinates.

AutoCAD LT 2000 has several ways to input co-ordinates to specify the length of objects or their angle of orientation. Co-ordinate input can also be used to specify the distance over which objects can be copied, moved or stretched. Gaps can be made in objects – e.g., by inputting the width of the gap in polar co-ordinates. Absolute, relative and polar co-ordinates are described below.

Absolute co-ordinates

This co-ordinate system relies on the location of the origin 0,0. The origin is normally located at the bottom left of the screen. The X and Y axis meet at the origin. An absolute co-ordinate is input as two numbers separated by a comma. The first number is the distance along the X axis and the second the distance on the Y axis. For example, to draw a line from the origin:

The @ symbol means 'from the last point'.

Command: L	(Type L and press Enter)
LINE specify first point: 0,0	(Type in the 0,0 press Enter)
Specify next point or [undo]: 100,100	(Type in the 100,100 press Enter)
To point:	(Press Enter to end the command)

Relative co-ordinates

This co-ordinate system relies on the location of the last point entered. The @ symbol is entered before the co-ordinate. It means from the last position. A co-ordinate @45,67 specifies a location 45 units along the X axis and 67 units along the Y axis *relative* to the last location.

You can only use the @ symbol during an AutoCAD LT 2000 command.

Polar co-ordinates

This co-ordinate system allows you to specify a distance and angle from the last point. It takes the format:

From the last point   Give as drawing units   Symbol for angle

@distance<n

Angle value between 0 and 360

Example: **@322<90**

Co-ordinate Input – Examples

You do not have to pick the first point of displacement on the object you are moving.

Polar co-ordinates can be used any time that AutoCAD LT asks for a displacement or a new point. To follow these examples, set a page size of 420 by 297 in decimal units.

Drawing a line – absolute and polar co-ordinates

Issue the Line command. Read the command line and enter an absolute co-ordinate of 0,0 and press Enter. A line runs from the origin out to the cross hairs.

In response to: 'Specify next point or [Undo]:' type in the polar co-ordinate @50<45. A line 50 mm long at an angle of 45 degrees is drawn. Continue with the following values in response to 'Specify next point or [Undo]:': @100<0, @200<90, @100<180, @100<270. Press Enter to finish the command.

If you accidentally terminate the current command, then use Object Snap to pick up from the end of the last line endpoint and proceed with the polar co-ordinates.

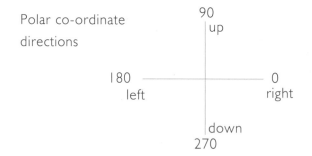

Polar co-ordinate directions

Moving a line by polar co-ordinates

Let's imagine you have to move the right vertical line 25mm to the right (0 degrees direction). Issue the Move command.

Click on the right vertical line when asked to 'Select objects'. Press Enter to tell AutoCAD LT 2000 that you have finished selecting objects.

Direction is input at an angle in polar co-ordinates.

In response to: 'Specify base point or displacement' click anywhere on the screen (click near the line). In response to: 'Specify second point of displacement' type in @25<0 and press Enter. The line is moved 25mm to the right.

Try doing this with the Copy command.

Using Zoom and Pan

Pan is one of the few commands where you do not need to look at the command line.

Zoom allows you to change the magnification of your view of the drawing. Pan allows you to move around the drawing without changing the magnification. Zoom and Pan are aids to help you work with the drawing.

Pan icon: just click on it, move out onto the drawing editor, hold down the left mouse button and drag. If you have a mouse with a wheel between the buttons try rotating this. When you are finished you must right-pick and click on Exit from the displayed menu.

You can pan and zoom by clicking on the right mouse button and selecting from the menu.

Zoom icon: click it and move onto the drawing, hold down the left mouse button and drag. When finished you must right-pick and click on Exit from the displayed menu.

Zoom window icon: this allows you to select a window or box around the area you want to magnify. Respond by selecting a point on the screen and pull a window around the objects you want to magnify.

If you get lost press the Esc key and try again.

Zoom previous icon: AutoCAD LT 2000 remembers the previous level of magnification and will return you to it when you click on the icon.

You can pan and zoom using the command line. Type zoom or z and pan or p and press Enter.

Exits from the Zoom and Pan options and blanks the command line

This command zooms to fit the entire drawing on the screen

Aerial View

Aerial view is especially useful if you are working on a drawing that occupies a large area. It enables you to view the whole drawing in a small window within the drawing editor. Panning and zooming in the smaller Aerial view window is reflected in the drawing editor.

The Aerial view window can be dragged around the screen, minimized, maximized and closed in the usual manner for all windows. Aerial view is found under the View menu: View > Aerial View.

The Aerial view can be called up by typing 'dsviewer' at the command line.

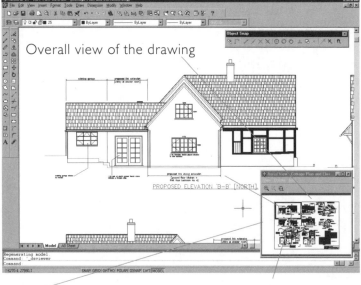

Overall view of the drawing

Aerial view is most useful for large complex drawings.

Area of the drawing shown in the drawing editor

Aerial view window

You cannot draw or edit inside the Aerial view window.

The Aerial view can immediately show changes made to the drawing in the drawing editor if the Dynamic Update is ticked under the Options menu on the Aerial view window

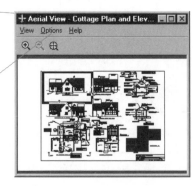

The Purge Command

To purge a drawing is to remove any references in the drawing to unused linetypes, text styles layers, Blocks, etc. A drawing that has been purged is often smaller in size and much more stable than an unpurged drawing.

A drawing that has never been purged can become unstable.

It is good practice to purge a drawing before you store it permanently or give it to another person. Always purge a drawing before sending via e-mail, for example.

While constructing a drawing you may make a layer or load a linetype and find that you never use it. Purge removes any references to them.

To issue the command

Type 'purge' at the command line and press Enter. A 'tree' view of the objects in the drawing is displayed. Select (that is, click to place a dot) the 'View items you can purge'.

Purge does not remove AutoCAD LT 2000's default settings such as the continuous linetype.

A plus sign shows that items under the selected heading can be purged. Click on the plus symbol to see the items

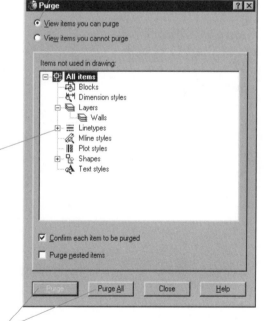

Purge does not delete anything that is used in the drawing.

Select the items to be purged and click on the Purge button or just click Purge All

How to Select Objects

Objects in the drawing editor need to be selected regularly while drawing and editing. Using the pickbox to select individual elements is a commonly used technique.

However, there are several other ways which are particularly useful for selecting several objects. Some of these methods are described here.

Imagine that the command line displays 'Select objects:' The following selection methods work:

Don't limit yourself to the same selection options all the time. Being familiar with several adds speed and accuracy to your work.

1 All: selects all objects in the drawing except those on layers that are thawed (see Chapter 7, *Working with Layers*). The complete drawing then highlights. This is useful if you wish to move the whole drawing to a new location on the page.

2 l: l is for last. The last object you worked on is selected.

3 p: p is for previous. The last objects you selected are selected.

4 f: f is for fence. You can select points on the screen through which AutoCAD LT draws a fence line. Objects over which the fence crosses are selected.

Cursor

Crossed lines are selected

Claret

Fence

5 cp: cp means crossing polygon. This time the 'fence' is called a polygon. Construct it the same way as the fence. Objects selected either cross the polygon or are completely inside it.

...cont'd

Don't bother pressing 'c' for a crossing window, just click and move the cursor from right to left for a crossing box.

6 c: c is for crossing. This selection method involves pulling a window around the objects. Those objects crossing the window or completely within it are selected. If you respond to the 'Select objects' prompt by just clicking a point on the drawing and moving to the left and up, a crossing selection window is formed automatically.

7 w: w is for window. Pull a window around the object(s). Those objects completely within the window are highlighted. If you don't respond to the 'select objects' prompt with 'w', just drag a window from right to left. This action automatically forms a selection window.

The crossing window is displayed with a dashed line; the window method shows a window displayed by a continuous line.

8 wp: this is a polygon window. Objects must be completely within the polygon for selection.

9 r: r is for remove. This invaluable option allows you to deselect objects that you accidentally select.

The crossing window is a dashed box

All the objects crossing the windows are selected along with those completely inside the window

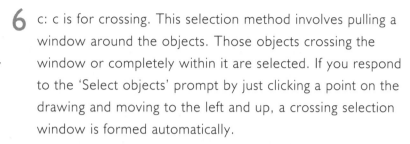

Liqueur   Sherry

You can mix the selection methods. For example, start with a crossing window and continue with a fence or a single click selection.

The complete selection window is a continuous box

Only this arc is selected

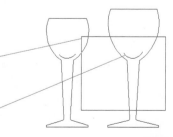

Grips – the Little Blue Boxes

You have probably experienced these little blue boxes appearing on objects in the drawing editor. They are called Grips. Pressing the Esc key removes them.

The Grips appear if you select an object while the command line is blank. They appear at specific points on an object such as the endpoints and midpoint of a line.

Grips can be dragged to perform actions such as rotating, moving or scaling an object.

Grips can be applied to several entities at once by dragging a window around them.

Grips on objects –
each square is a Grip

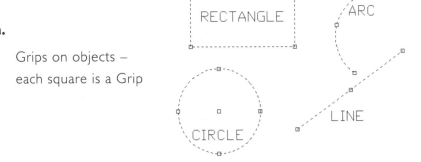

Right-clicking when a Grip is highlighted brings up the commands associated with the Grip.

To call up the Grips dialog box, use Format > Options and choose the Selection tab.

A tick here allows the Grips to function

Sets the colour for selected and unselected Grips

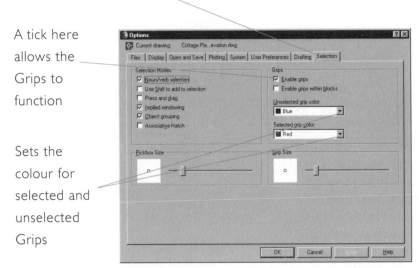

How to Use the Grips

Grips allow you to apply the following commands to an object: Stretch, Move, Rotate, Scale and Mirror. To practise these options, draw a separate line and circle.

Cycle through the Grip options by pressing either the Spacebar or the Enter key.

Moving a circle with Grips
Without issuing a command, click on the circle. Grips then appear. Now click on the centre-point Grip: it changes to a solid colour (red is the default). The command line shows:

STRETCH

Specify stretch point or [Base point/Copy/Undo/eXit]:

To see the other commands press the Spacebar or the Enter key. Keep pressing the key until you see the Move command. The command line then shows:

Specify move point[Base point/Copy/Undo/eXit]:

The default option is shown in angled brackets. When you move the cursor, the circle moves with it. At this point you can do one of three things:

- Click a point on the screen to reposition the circle
- Use polar co-ordinates to re-locate the circle accurately
- Use Object Snap to snap to another object

To remove the Grips, press the Esc key twice.

Use polar co-ordinates or Object Snap in conjunction with Grips for greater accuracy.

Stretching a line with Grips
Select the line. The Grips will appear. Click on one of the endpoints to highlight a Grip. Press the Spacebar or the Enter key until you find:

STRETCH

Specify stretch point[Base point/Copy/Undo/eXit]:

At this point you can do one of three things:

- Click a point on the screen to stretch the line
- Use polar co-ordinates to stretch the line a specific distance
- Use Object Snap to snap to another object

System Variables

System variables hold specific settings or values that affect how AutoCAD LT works. By changing a variable you specify how a command might function or how the AutoCAD LT screen looks. Here are some useful variables.

In AutoCAD LT Release 1 and 2, the Blipmode system variable is set to 'On' as the default.

Blipmode

This controls the display of small '+' symbols called Blips, at selection points on the screen. It is set to 'Off' in AutoCAD LT 97 and 98. Try switching it on and draw a line to see the effect. At the command line type 'Blipmode' and press the Spacebar or Enter key. Type 'On' or 'Off'. The default setting is shown in angled brackets.

Blips are not part of the drawing. They are not printed. The Redraw command (or just R and Enter) removes Blips.

Mirrtext

If AutoCAD LT 2000 is not working the way that you have come to expect, check the system variables. Someone may have changed one.

This variable controls how text is mirrored when you use the Mirror command. If text is mirrored when the variable is set to 1 (the default value), the text appears inverted (exactly as it would appear in a real mirror).

If the Mirrtext variable is set to 0, the text appears normal (legible). Type 'Mirrtext' at the command line to change it.

Ucsicon

The image of the X and Y axis at the bottom left of the screen is controlled by this system variable. It can be switched on or off by typing 'Ucsicon' at the command line.

Filedia

Controls the display of the dialog boxes associated with file commands such as the Save and Save As. There are two settings – 1 causes the boxes to be displayed (this is the default); 0 prevents their display. If a dialog box is not displayed you must read the command line to save the files. Type 'Filedia' to change the settings.

Users of the pre-AutoCAD LT 98 release will find the variables work the same way.

Offsetdist

Allows you to set a default value for the offset command. Type 'Offsetdist' and type a new value in drawing units.

Advanced Drawing Commands

In this chapter, you'll learn how to use some of AutoCAD LT 2000's more advanced commands to create complex objects. Construction lines such as rays and xlines help you to place objects on the drawing more accurately. They are designed to be quick to draw. The commands for creating polyline curves, circles and straight line segments are also examined in detail. Lastly you can learn how to draw a door arc as it might be constructed in an architectural drawing.

Covers

Chapter Four

Ray

Rays can be constructed using different linetypes such as dotted or dash-dot (see *Linetypes*, page 92).

How the command works

A ray is a line that has a starting point and extends off to infinity in a single direction.

Ray lines are used to help construct a drawing rather than be objects as a part of the drawing.

When the command is issued, AutoCAD LT asks for the ray's starting point and then for another point through which the ray will run.

Command line: ray

Menu: Draw > Ray

Toolbar:

The command in action

When the command is issued the response is:

Right-clicking with the mouse over the drawing editor allows you to repeat the last command.

From point: Specify start point. You can use Object Snap or type an absolute co-ordinate.

Through point: Specify through point. You can use Object Snap or type a polar co-ordinate.

Finish the command by pressing Enter, the Spacebar, or clicking the right mouse button.

The properties associated with a ray can be modified using the command Ddmodify.

Rays emanating from a point. Rays have an endpoint for Object Snap but no midpoint.

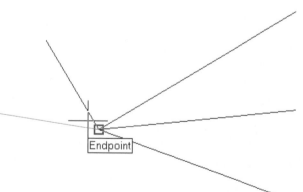

Construction Line or Xline

You can snap to the root of the xline using the Object Snap midpoint.

How the command works

A construction or xline is a line that runs to infinity in two directions. As in the construction of any type of line you need two points to define it.

The first point you pick becomes the 'root' of the construction line. There are many ways to pick the points for constructing the xline, including the Object Snap modes.

Command line: xline, or the alias 'xl'

Menu: Draw > Construction Line

Toolbar:

The command in action

When the command is issued you have to select the first point or root. The default is to just pick a point on the screen or use Object Snap.

Five other options are offered. To select one of these options, type the capitalized letter from the list. The options are shown below:

Use construction lines sparingly, otherwise your drawing can quickly become cluttered with lines.

Constructs a horizontal or vertical xline. Use Object Snap to draw it through a specific point

Draws the xline parallel to an existing line – decide the distance

XLINE Specify a point or [Hor/Ver/Ang/Bisect/Offset]:

Default option – pick a point or use Object Snap

Specify an angle for the xline

Bisect an existing angle

Specify through point: Select a point. You can use Object Snap or type a polar co-ordinate. To finish the command press the Enter key or Spacebar.

Double Line – Overview

How the command works

A double line consists of two parallel lines and can be used, for example, to represent cavity walls in a building. You can tell AutoCAD LT how far apart the two lines are from each other. When drawing a double line, select beginning and end points in the usual way. Double lines can have caps at either end or none at all. All the lines that compose a double line can be edited and erased independently.

You can enter the width of a double line either before or after you select the start point.

Command line: dline, or the alias 'dl'

Menu: Draw > Double Line

Toolbar:

Each of these double lines are drawn from left to right

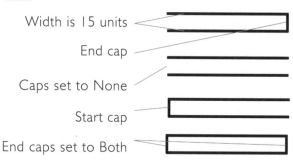

Width is 15 units

End cap

Caps set to None

Start cap

End caps set to Both

The most useful options are Width, Caps and Break.

The command in action

When the command is issued the response is:

Specify start point or [Break/Caps/Dragline/Offset/Snap/ Undo/Width]

Note how two of the options begin with 'C' so you have to type the first two letters to distinguish them.

The default option is to pick a point (use Object Snap if you wish). To input a width type W and press Enter.

The value you input is in drawing units. Once the first point is selected the command line options change to:

Specify next point or [Arc/Break/CAps/CLose/Dragline/Snap/ Undo/Width]

Continue selecting points. Press Enter to finish.

Double Line Options in Detail

Break/Caps/Dragline/Offset/Snap/Undo/Width/:

The Offset option allows you to start the double line a specific distance from some object or base point.

Break

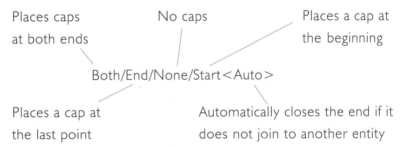

If Break is ON the caps are removed

This horizontal double line was drawn with Caps set to none

If Break is OFF the join appears

Caps

Places caps at both ends

No caps

Places a cap at the beginning

The Snap option allows you to snap to an existing object.

Both/End/None/Start<Auto>

Places a cap at the last point

Automatically closes the end if it does not join to another entity

Dragline

Because double lines have a distance between them, you need to tell AutoCAD LT how the two lines are constructed when you snap to the end or midpoint of other entities. The Dragline option allows this.

The Undo option allows segments of what you have drawn to be removed while remaining in the command.

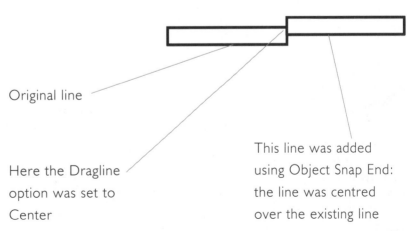

Original line

Here the Dragline option was set to Center

This line was added using Object Snap End: the line was centred over the existing line

Polylines

The Close option draws the polyline back to the first point picked. It has special editing properties.

How the command works

Polylines are quite special. Unlike the standard line they can have a width and they can follow a curved path. Polylines need special editing in order to be modified.

To draw the polyline you need to give it a start and end point. Other options such as the width must be selected after the first point is chosen.

You can give different widths for the beginning and end points of a polyline: AutoCAD LT tapers the line from one width to the other. Polylines can also be turned into curves.

Command line: pline, or the alias 'pl'

Menu: Draw > Polyline

Toolbar:

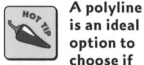

A polyline is an ideal option to choose if you want to create arrowheads.

The command in action

When the command is issued the response is:

Specify start point: Pick in the usual way.

Arc/Close/Halfwidth/Length/Undo/Width/<Endpoint of line>:

Select the Width option. Type a beginning width. Press Enter and type in an end width. Try drawing a few lines.

You can specify a halfwidth – this is the width from the central axis of the polyline to the edge.

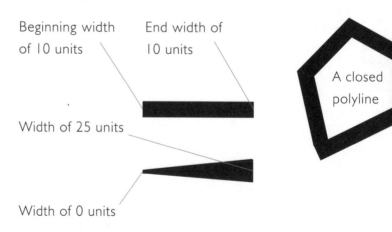

Beginning width of 10 units

End width of 10 units

Width of 25 units

Width of 0 units

A closed polyline

Polyline Shapes

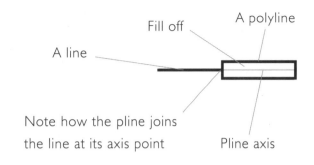

A line   Fill off   A polyline

Note how the pline joins the line at its axis point

Pline axis

Width = 0   Width = 10

Width = 10

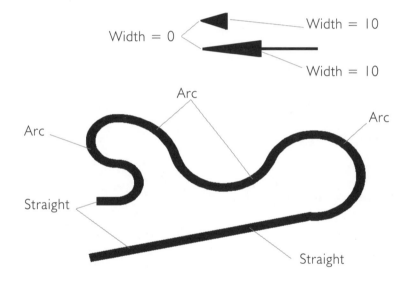

Arc

Arc

Arc

Straight

Straight

The Length option allows a polyline to be increased by entering a value in units.

The prompt is 'Length of line:'

Just type a value and AutoCAD LT extends the line at the same angle as the existing polyline.

This shape was drawn with one execution of the command. The width was changed after each segment was drawn. The starting and ending width of each segment is the same.

Rectangles

How the command works

A rectangle is composed of four polylines. You simply pick two points to draw it. The sides of the rectangle are always parallel to the horizontal and vertical sides of the screen.

Command line: rectang

Menu: Draw > Rectangle

Toolbar:

The command in action

Issue the command. Pick two points:

You can Object Snap to the sides of the rectangle.

Pick point 1   Pick point 2

3D Polyline and Rectangle

3D polylines are similar to the standard pline. The differences are: (1) they're drawn in 3D space and so can take a Z co-ordinate, and (2) they can only be converted to special types of curves.

Command line: pline, or the alias 'pl'

Menu: Draw > Polyline

Toolbar: None

The command in action

When the command is issued the response is:

Specify start point of polyline: Pick as usual
Specify Endpoint of line:

When you press Enter to end the command, AutoCAD LT offers an option to close the polyline.

Polygons

Polygons are made from polylines. You can edit them using the pedit command.

How the command works

A polygon is an enclosed shape with 3 to 1024 sides. You can draw a polygon in two basic ways.

Define one side of the polygon and AutoCAD LT draws the others; or pick the centre of the polygon and AutoCAD LT draws the sides inside or outside of a circle.

Command line: polygon, or the alias 'pg'

Menu: Draw > Polygon

Toolbar:

The command in action

Issue the command. AutoCAD LT needs to know the number of sides you want in the polygon.

You can Object Snap a line onto the mid-point or end point of the sides of the polyline.

Type in a value and press Enter. The response is:

Specify centre of polygon or [Edge]:(Press Enter to accept Edge)

Enter an option [Inscribed in circle/Circumscribed about circle]<I>:

This is an inscribed 5 sided polygon

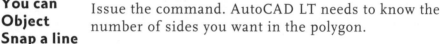

Even though a polygon can be defined around or inside a circle, you cannot Object Snap to the centre of a polygon.

The radius can be input as a value or picked with the cursor

This is a circumscribed 5 sided polygon

This is a 5 sided polygon from a straight edge

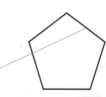

Arcs

How the command works

There are many ways to draw an arc, each of which is listed on the drop-down menu below. Arcs are parts of circles, and all arcs have a beginning and an end point. AutoCAD LT uses these points in three techniques. All arcs have a centre: this is used in four techniques. Three techniques use an angle to specify the distance the arc spans.

Command line: arc

Menu: Draw > Arc   New in

Toolbar: LT 98

Arc Options

3 Points
Start, Center, End
Start, Center, Angle
Start, Center, Length
Start, End, Angle
Start, End, Direction
Start, End, Radius
Center, Start, End
Center, Start, Angle
Center, Start, Length
Continue

Arcs are made from a circle. Three points are needed for AutoCAD LT to draw the arc.

The command in action

Here are two of the techniques:

1 The Start, Center, End option.

Start, Center, End

The arc is drawn anticlockwise

Arcs can be a bit difficult to master. Concentrate on one (perhaps the Start Center, End) until you can predict the results.

2 The Start, Center, Angle option.

Start, Center, Angle

The angle is specified by where you pick

Negative angles give a clockwise arc

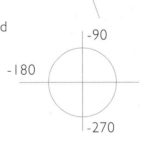

-90

-180

-270

How to Draw a Door Arc

This is the type of arc that is used by an architect to describe the sweep of a door.

 An angle that is negative sweeps an arc clockwise.

To follow this, set up a drawing using decimal units with a sheet size of about 2000mm by 2000mm. Use double lines to draw a wall and a single line to represent the door at 90 degrees to the wall. The door gap must also be 900mm. The arc is drawn using the options Start, Center, Angle.

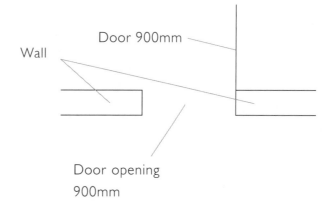

Wall

Door 900mm

Door opening 900mm

 Use the Object Snap modes to position the arc Start and Center points.

Command sequence
Click Start, Center, Angle.

Pick the start point using the Object Snap End command to locate the top of the door.

 The angle option is used to describe the distance the arc sweeps.

For the centre, pick where the door meets the wall using Object Snap Midpoint.

When asked for the angle, type in 90. This setting sweeps an arc anticlockwise through a distance of 90 degrees.

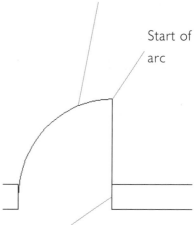

Angle is 90 (anticlockwise)

Start of arc

Centre of the circle that makes the arc Midpoint

Donuts

If you erase a donut (or other object), other parts of the drawing may appear to have also been erased. Type 'r' for Redraw, and AuotCAD LT refreshes/redraws the screen: you should see the unerased objects reappear.

How the command works

Donuts are circles made from polylines. Donuts have two diameters. The area between the diameters is filled solid if the Fill command is set to 'On'.

Command line: donut, or the alias 'do'

Menu: Draw > Donut

Toolbar:

The command in action

AutoCAD LT asks for the inside and outside diameters. The default options are shown in angled brackets.

The centre point can be picked using Object Snap or by just clicking on it. The Donut command continues until you press the Enter key or Spacebar to finish.

You must type 'Regen' after you change the Fill command. This allows you to see the effect on the donuts (or polylines).

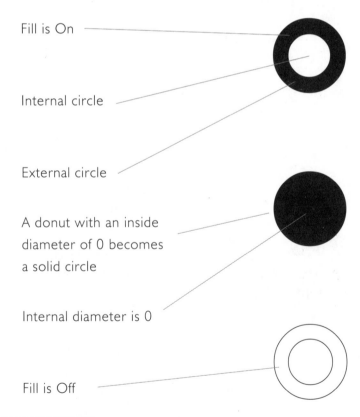

Fill is On

Internal circle

External circle

A donut with an inside diameter of 0 becomes a solid circle

Internal diameter is 0

Fill is Off

Splines

How the command works

A spline is a curve. To create a spline, pick several points on the screen. AutoCAD LT then draws the curve through the first and last points, and as close as possible to the points in between.

Command line: spline

Menu: Draw > Spline

Toolbar:

The command in action

You are asked for each point. Pick the points in the usual way and press Enter three times to end the command. The splines below were drawn with different tolerances. To try it: draw two lines – one vertical and one horizontal.

Different Techniques:

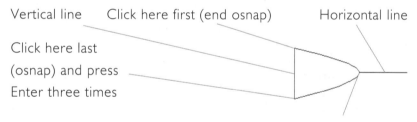

Vertical line   Click here first (end osnap)   Horizontal line

Click here last (osnap) and press Enter three times

Click here (end osnap) and type 't' for tolerance. Set the tolerance to 0 and Enter)

Carry out the same procedure here but change the tolerance to 25

Change the tolerance here to 50

Notice how the spline always goes through the first and last point picked. It 'attempts' to go through the second point when the tolerance is above o (zero).

Ellipses

How the command works

An ellipse has a long (or major) axis and a short (or minor) axis. AutoCAD LT draws an ellipse by asking you to select or specify the length of the axes. Whichever is the longest is the major axis.

AutoCAD LT takes the longest axis as the major and the shorter axis as the minor one.

In other words, you don't have to say which is major or minor: AutoCAD LT just lets you draw.

Command line: ellipse, or the alias 'el'

Menu: Draw > Ellipse

Toolbar:

The command in action

The command line default prompt is ':<Axis endpoint 1>:' Once the point is picked you have set the centre of the ellipse.

The prompt now asks for the 'Axis endpoint 2'. This determines the length of the first axis. The prompt for '<Other axis distance>' describes the ellipse fully.

The length of the axis can be input as polar co-ordinates.

This becomes the minor axis in this example

At this stage the prompt is: 'Other axis distance'

The 'Center' option allows you to pick the centre of the ellipse first. You then need to tell AutoCAD LT the length of the axes.

If you draw in Isometric mode you can create isocircles. These are really ellipses pretending to be circles viewed at an angle.

How to Edit Objects

In this chapter, we introduce many of AutoCAD LT 2000's powerful editing commands. After mastering these commands you can appreciate that most of your time working on a drawing is spent editing objects onscreen.

Covers

Chapter Five

Erase and the Revision Cloud

See pages 36 and 37 on how to select objects.

How the command works

Erase removes objects from a drawing. To use Erase efficiently, you must master the art of object selection. Objects selected to be erased are shown highlighted. If you want to erase part of an object, use a command like Break to split the object in two. Press Enter to finish.

Command line: erase, or the alias 'e'

Menu: Modify > Erase

Toolbar:

If you select one object too many with the Erase command, you can type U to undo the selection and still stay in the command.

The command in action

Issue the Erase command. Select the objects and press Enter to finish the command. Remember you can mix the selection methods.

Highlighted objects are erased

when you press Enter

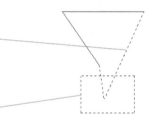

Crossing selection box is used here

Revision Cloud with a small arc

Revision Cloud – AutoCAD LT 98 and 2000 only

When viewing a plotted drawing, you may 'mark' a section to be revised with a pen or pencil. You can simulate this procedure in AutoCAD LT using the Revision Cloud. A Revision Cloud is drawn using arcs.

Command line: revcloud

Toolbar:

You can specify the arc size (use A and Enter to select the option) and simply draw the cloud by moving the pointing device. AutoCAD LT closes the cloud once you near the beginning.

Revision Cloud with a large arc

Copy Objects around the Drawing

 If you want to copy an object to a very specific location in the drawing, use Object Snap to pick up the object and Object Snap to position it.

How the command works

Copy works in a very similar way to move. AutoCAD LT asks you to select the object(s) you want to copy and then the base point for picking the objects up, and finally the place where you want to position the objects. If you want to make several copies of an object, use the Multiple option. In Multiple mode, AutoCAD LT allows you to place as many copies in the drawing as you wish.

Command line: copy, or the alias 'cp'

Menu: Modify > Copy

Toolbar:

The command in action

Issue the Copy command. Select the objects and press Enter to finish the selection. Remember, you can mix the selection methods. Pick a base point on or near the objects to copy and select the second point in a similar way.

Copy the circle
so its centre is
on the mid-point
of the line

 If you're using the same text in several positions on the drawing, use Copy with the Multiple option to make any number of copies of the text.

Select
the
circle

Midpoint

Base point is the
center of the circle
– use Object Snap

Second base point is the
mid-point of the line – use
Object Snap Midpoint

Mirror

If you mirror objects with Ortho on, you can only mirror at 90 or 180 degrees. This can be very useful. Try it, and when asked for the second mirror axis point, click with the mouse to lock the image.

Mirror is a Grips option. Highlight a Grip and press the Spacebar until you see Mirror (see page 39 for more information on using Grips).

If you don't want the text inverted when you mirror, then change the system variable Mirrtext to 0 before you issue the command. See page 40 on *System Variables*.

How the command works

The command is used to mirror object(s) across an axis. You select the object you want to mirror, tell AutoCAD LT where the mirror axis is and AutoCAD LT does the rest. The command has two interesting features. Firstly you don't actually have to have an axis drawn on the screen: you can use any two points which define an axis. Secondly you can tell AutoCAD LT to delete the object(s) you're going to mirror so that you end up with one inverted copy.

Command line: mirror, or the alias 'mi'

Menu: Modify > Mirror

Toolbar:

The command in action

Issue the Mirror command. Select the objects you want and press Enter to finish the selection. Remember, you can mix the selection methods. The mirror axis is defined by any two points on the line. Pick the points when AutoCAD LT asks: 'Specify first point of mirror line' and 'Specify second point of mirror line'. If you accept the default to 'Delete source objects? [Yes/No]<N>:' the objects will be mirrored.

Use Object Snap to pick points on the mirror axis

In this case the mirror axis was defined between the Midpoints of the top and bottom horizontal lines

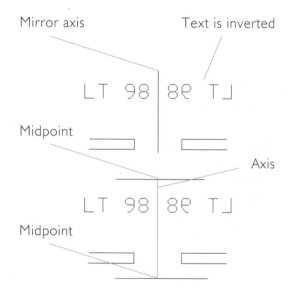

Mirror axis

Text is inverted

Midpoint

Axis

Midpoint

Offset

Polylines are offset from the axis that runs down through the centre of the pline.

How the command works

Offset makes a copy of objects parallel to existing objects. Offset is one of the most useful commands in AutoCAD LT and is well worth mastering.

AutoCAD needs to know:

´ What you want to offset

- The distance to offset

- The side of the original object from which you want the offset to occur

Command line: offset, or the alias 'of'

Menu: Modify > Offset

Toolbar:

AutoCAD LT keeps the last offset distance as the default.

The command in action

Issue the Offset command. AutoCAD LT immediately asks for the distance you want to offset – 'Specify offset distance or [Through] <Through>:'

Enter a distance and select the object. You can only select one object to offset at a time. Finally select the side from which to offset the object.

If you offset a polyline make sure that the offset distance is more than the halfwidth distance of the polyline, otherwise you won't see it.

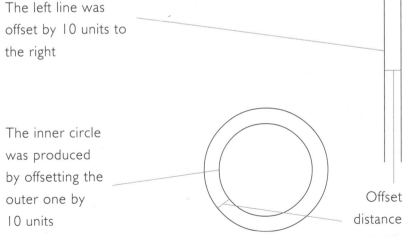

The left line was offset by 10 units to the right

The inner circle was produced by offsetting the outer one by 10 units

Offset distance

Rotate

How the command works
You can rotate any object(s) around a central rotation point. First select the objects to rotate. Then specify the base point about which you want the rotation to occur (which can be on the object itself).

Rotate is a Grips option. Highlight a Grip and press the Spacebar until you see Rotate (see page 39).

Lastly set the angle through which rotation should occur. A positive rotation angle means anticlockwise. A negative angle is clockwise.

Command line: rotate, or the alias 'ro'

Menu: Modify > Rotate

Toolbar:

The command in action
Issue the Rotate command. Select the objects and press Enter to finish the selection. You can mix the selection methods.

Now AutoCAD LT asks for the 'Specify base point:'. Pick a point. Type a value in response to the prompt for 'Specify rotation angle or [Reference]'.

Original position of
the object(s)

The reference angle allows a rotation from an existing angle – usually of the object being rotated.

Base point about which
rotation occurs

The cursor is attached to this base point. As it is moved, the objects rotate. Type an angle if you wish or just click on a point on the screen

Scale

Scale is a Grips option. Highlight a Grip and press the Spacebar until you see Scale (see page 39).

How the command works

Objects can be scaled up or down from a base point. A scale value of 1 leaves the object as it is.

A value of 0.5 halves its size while a value of 2 doubles it.

Command line: scale, or the alias 'sc'

Menu: Modify > Scale

Toolbar:

The command in action

Issue the Scale command. Select the objects and press Enter to finish the selection.

You can mix the selection methods. The base option can be on or near the object. Object Snap may also be used.

If you scale an object that has been dimensioned, the value of the dimension changes only if associative dimensioning is switched on.

Text while being scaled is highlighted

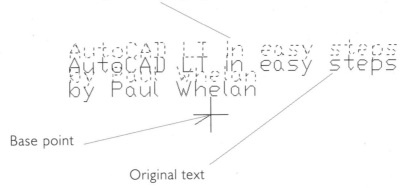

Base point

Original text

A scaled object increases or decreases its size from the select base point.

The Scale command should not be used to produce a drawing on the correct size before it is printed. The Print command has a separate Plotting Scale option.

Stretch

Polar co-ordinates are very useful in stretching. In the example here, you could stretch the lines by 10 units by entering @10<0 when asked for the 'Second point of displacement'.

How the command works

The Stretch command either lengthens or shortens objects. A crossing window must cross the objects you want to stretch. Any object that lies completely within the selection window is moved. AutoCAD LT asks you for a base point that it uses to calculate the amount of stretch.

Command line: Stretch

Menu: Modify > Stretch

Toolbar:

The command in action

Issue the Stretch command. Select the objects by pulling a crossing window so that it cuts or crosses the object you want to stretch.

Select objects:	Pull a crossing window or crossing polygon from right to left
Base point of displacement:	Pick a point on/near the object
Second point of displacement:	Click a point with the cursor or use co-ordinates or Object Snap to another object

Objects completely inside the selection box are not stretched – only moved.

1 │ Lines to be stretched
4870.0359

2 End — Crossing objects
4870.0359
Crossing pickbox
Start

If you do not use a crossing window or polygon you cannot stretch objects.

3
7400.9207

Stretched objects – note the changed dimension

Lengthen

If an object is closed – like a double line or a polyline – it cannot be lengthened.

You can use Lengthen to find the existing length of an object. Issue the command and select the object. AutoCAD LT tells you its length.

How the command works

This command allows you to increase or decrease the length of objects. Select the objects then tell AutoCAD LT how you want to increase/decrease the length of the objects.

Several interesting options are available. You can lengthen an object by a percentage or by a specific amount. You may also tell AutoCAD LT an overall length for an object and it will modify the object to match that length.

Command line: lengthen, or the alias 'len'

Menu: Modify > Lengthen

Toolbar:

The command in action

To try this command with the Delta option, draw a line 4 units long. You can increase or decrease it by 3 units. Issue the Lengthen command. All the options are displayed:

Select an orbject or [DElta/Percent/Total/DYnamic]:

If you select an object now, AutoCAD LT simply tells you its length and then returns you to the options. You must select an option to change an object's length.

Type DE for the Delta option. This allows you to change the object's length by 3 units (-3 decreases it; +3 increases it). The prompt changes to:

Note how two of the options begin with 'D' so you have to type the first two letters to distinguish them.

Enter delta length or [Angle]<0.0>:type in a length and press

                          Enter

Select the object to change [Undo]:

Be careful as to which part of the entity you select. Click near to the end at which you want the change to occur. Press Enter to finish the command. Try each of the other options yourself.

Trim

How the command works

Trim allows you to clip off pieces of objects that intersect with other objects. Think of the Trim command as a pair of scissors that cut along an edge (called a cutting edge).

AutoCAD LT asks you for a cutting edge. Once you do this, it needs to know which objects you want to trim. After you select these, the command trims the objects you chose.

Command line: trim, or the alias 'tr'

Menu: Modify > Trim

Toolbar:

The command in action

Issue the Trim command. Select the objects along which you want to cut or trim when asked:

Select cutting edges: This is actually one phrase. Read it as:
Select objects: 'Select the objects you want to form the
                        cutting edge'.
Select objects to trim: Select the object(s) you want.

Press Enter to finish the command.

If you select the wrong cutting edge, just type 'u' and press Enter. AutoCAD LT then leaves you 'in' the command and you can select new objects.

Trim allows you to select several cutting edges at the same time.

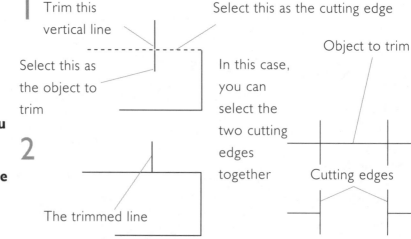

Trim this vertical line

Select this as the cutting edge

Select this as the object to trim

Object to trim

In this case, you can select the two cutting edges together

Cutting edges

2

The trimmed line

Extend

How the command works

With Extend, you can extend the length of an object to meet another object. The object to which you are extending is called the boundary. You cannot extend objects which are parallel because they never meet.

Command line: extend, or the alias 'ex'

Menu: Modify > Extend

Toolbar:

The command in action

Issue the Extend command. Select the boundary you want to extend to in the usual way when AutoCAD LT prompts:

Select boundary edges: This is actually one phrase.

Select objects: Read it as: 'Select the objects you want to form the boundary edge'

Boundary edge

Line to extend

Boundary edge selected

Pickbox selecting the line you want to extend

Note that the pickbox is near the end you want to extend

 When AutoCAD LT asks you to select the object to extend, you must click on the side of the object near the boundary, otherwise AutoCAD LT tells you there is no boundary in the other direction.

Chamfer

Polyline, Angle, Trim and Method should be explored only after you have mastered the basic technique of applying a distance.

How the command works

Chamfer joins two lines by adding a third line. The easiest way to understand the command is to apply it to two lines joining at a right angle. AutoCAD LT needs to know how much of each line is to be removed (called the chamfer distance) before the third line is drawn to join the ends.

Command line: chamfer, or the alias 'cha'

Menu: Modify > Chamfer

Toolbar:

The command in action

Issue the Chamfer command. The following options are displayed:

Select first line [Polyline/Distance/Angle/Trim/Method]:

Before you select the line, check the distance by typing 'd'.

When the chamfer distances are input, the command automatically finishes. Issue the command again and then apply the chamfer.

1 You must input two chamfer distances. The first one applies to the first line you pick.

2 In both these cases the chamfer distance 1 was 30 units and the second distance was 10 units.

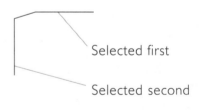

Selected first

Selected second

Chamfer distance 1

Chamfer distance 2

Chamfer line

If both chamfer distances are set to 0, the two lines are joined with a standard intersection.

Selected second.

Selected first

Fillet

A fillet radius of 0 brings about the intersection of two lines, even if they were never 'filleted' before.

How the command works

Fillet puts a curve on a sharp corner. The curve is actually an arc. AutoCAD LT asks you for a radius for the arc.

Once this is input the command finishes automatically. Issue the command again and apply the radius you input.

Command line: fillet, or the alias 'f'

Menu: Modify > Fillet

Toolbar:

The command in action

Two non-parallel lines can be extended to intersect by applying a fillet radius of 0 to them.

Issue the Fillet command. Type 'r' to select the radius option. Type in a value and press Enter. The command then ends.

Right-click the mouse to call up the floating menu. Select 'Repeat Fillet' and select lines to apply the radius you entered.

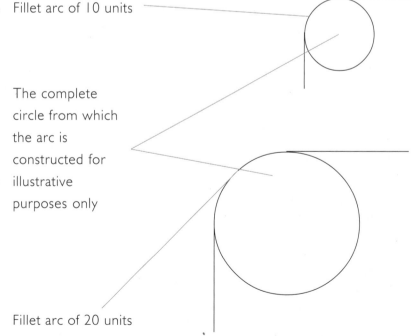

Fillet arc of 10 units

The complete circle from which the arc is constructed for illustrative purposes only

Fillet arc of 20 units

Fillet is like chamfer in that the command needs to be run twice; once to input the arc radius and the second time to apply it.

Break

When AutoCAD LT asks you to select the object, it is also asking you to select the first break point.

How the command works

Break carries out several interesting actions on an object. Take for example, a line: the AutoCAD LT Break command allows you to create a gap in the line or erase a section of a line.

It also allows you to put an invisible break point on a line. Two points are selected on the object and AutoCAD LT then removes the section of the object between them.

Command line: break, or the alias 'br'

Menu: Modify > Break

Toolbar:

The command in action

Try this command on a line. Issue the Break command. AutoCAD LT responds with:

Select object: Pick a point on the line

Specify second break point or [First point]:   Pick a second point

Line before applying
the Break command

If you do not want to use the first point you selected as a break point just type 'f' and press Enter. AutoCAD LT then lets you pick a new point.

Point selected when
asked to 'Select
object'

The gap created

Point selected when asked 'Enter second point'

Break – Examples in Action

Using Break to erase part of the line
Pick a point on the line and then pick a point off the end of the line:

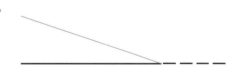

Point selected when asked to 'Select object'

This section is erased

Point selected off the end of the line when asked 'Enter second point'

Making an invisible break
Pick a point on the line. In response to: 'Specify second point', type in the @ symbol. AutoCAD LT then inserts an invisible break.

An invisible break is one that is not seen when the drawing it plotted/ printed.

Point selected when asked to 'Select object'

When asked to 'Enter second point', type '@' and press Enter

You can check to see if an invisible break has occurred by using the Erase command. Part of the line up to the invisible break highlights.

Using polar co-ordinates with Break
When AutoCAD LT asks for 'Enter second point', type in a polar co-ordinate distance and angle. In the case of this horizontal line, a value like @12<0 creates a gap 12 units wide.

Arrays

A row is horizontal; a column is vertical.

Users of releases previous to LT 98 don't have this dialog box. All entries must be made at the command line prompts.

Rectangular Arrays start at the bottom left of the screen and are calculated up and towards the right.

How the command works

Array produces copies of objects either in rows or columns or around a central point (Polar Array). In the rectangular Array, you need to select the objects to be arrayed and tell AutoCAD LT the number of columns and rows and the distance between them.

In the Polar Array you select a point around which the Array is created.

Command line: array, or the alias 'ar'

Menu: Modify > Array

Toolbar:

The command in action

A Polar Array is considered here to array a triangle. Issue the command. The Array dialog box is displayed.

Click here for a Polar Array   Select the object to be arrayed
                                     – in this case a triangle

Pick the centre point of the Array

The width and height of the objects being Arrayed must be taken into consideration when entering the distance between rows and columns in a rectangular Array.

Enter 24 here

Click to see a preview of the Arrayed object(s)

When the preview is shown AutoCAD LT prompts you to Accept or Modify the Array. Selecting Modify returns you to the dialog box.

Center of the Array

Text, Points and Units

In this chapter, you'll learn how to place text on a drawing. Editing of the text, including the use of the spell checker, is also covered. The old problem of selecting a text size for plotting/printing is tackled concisely on page 77. The use of the drawing object's points and the various point styles are also covered in detail. And lastly, we will look at how you can control the setup and display of units in the Units Control dialog box.

Covers

Chapter Six

Using Single Line Text

Introduction to text commands

Text is very important in precision drawings such as those produced by AutoCAD LT. Text is an object on a drawing, just as a line or a circle is an object. This implies that it is open to the same editing commands such as Scale, Move and Erase. AutoCAD LT allows you to use many different styles of text. You can also create a style yourself from the given fonts.

Text is an entity that can be scaled, moved, mirrored, etc.

Single Line Text

At times you will need to just put a line of text on the drawing for the purpose of annotation. For this, use the Single Line Text command. If you need to place several lines of text on the drawing use the Multiline Text editor.

How the command works

AutoCAD LT asks you to click on a start point for the text. A cursor displays at that point. You then type the text and press Enter to move to the next line or press Enter again to finish the command. The options available allow you to justify the text (left, right or centre) or apply a style. Once a point is selected you must supply the text height and the angle of orientation.

Command: dtext, or the alias 'dt'

Menu: Draw > Single Line Text

Pressing the Spacebar inserts a space while in the 'Text' option. Normally in AutoCAD LT, it is the equivalent of pressing the Enter key.

The command in action

Issue the Single Line Text command. Select a start point. Enter a height. This height can be clicked with the cursor. AutoCAD LT offers you the last height you used as the default. A rotation angle of 0 means the text is horizontal. At the prompt 'Text', type in the text you want. This is one of the few instances where pressing the Spacebar does in fact insert a space and is not interpreted as 'Enter'.

Start or insertion point   Standard text font

AutoCAD LT in easy steps
by Paul Whelan

Paragraph Text

 The first time this command is run, AutoCAD LT has to 'initialise' the editor. This may take a few seconds, so be patient.

How the command works

Use this text option to place several concurrent lines of text in a drawing. When the command is issued, AutoCAD LT asks you to specify the corners of a box.

The text you type fills the box. AutoCAD LT opens a small word processor for you to insert and edit your text.

Command: mtext, or the alias 'mt'

Menu: Draw > Paragraph Text

Toolbar: A

The command in action

Issue the Paragraph Text command. Pick a 'first' and 'opposite' corner to show AutoCAD LT where you want the text positioned. The Multiline Text Editor opens:

The current font

Click here for other fonts

Font size

Holds special characters, like the degree or diameter symbol

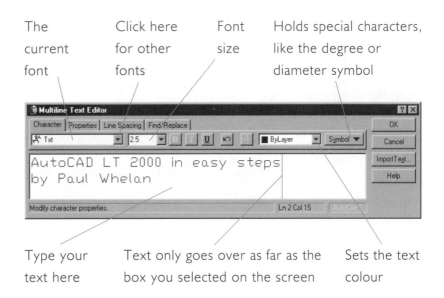

Type your text here

Text only goes over as far as the box you selected on the screen

Sets the text colour

Click on OK when you have finished with the editor.

Multiline Text Editor Options

The Style option under the Properties tab contains the STANDARD style only, unless you have already defined some styles.

The Character, Properties, Line Spacing and Find/Replace tabs lead into many options within the Multiline Text Editor. The Properties tab is shown below.

Positions text within the box. Select text by dragging over it, then select the desired justification option here

Allows you to change the width of the text box

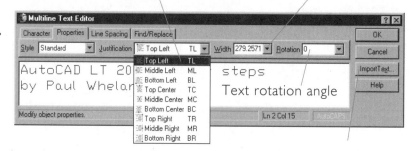

Text rotation angle

Rich Text Format (.rtf extension) retains the formatting of text and is an option usually available under the Save As command in most word processors.

Imports a text document written outside of AutoCAD LT 2000

When you choose the Import Text button, the 'Open' dialog box displays, allowing you to examine folders to find the desired text file. Most word processors can save files in the RTF (Rich Text Format). This is an ideal format to use for files that you may want to import into AutoCAD LT.

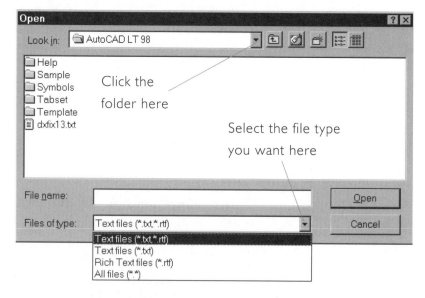

Click the folder here

Select the file type you want here

You can only import files up to 16K in size.

The Spell Checker

The spell checker can be called up by typing spell or the alias 'sp' on the command line.

The spell checker is found under the Tools drop-down menu.

Menu: Tools > Spelling

Toolbar: if   if customised

The suggested word. If this is not correct, select the word you want from the list or type the desired word here

Click here to ignore all occurrences of the word

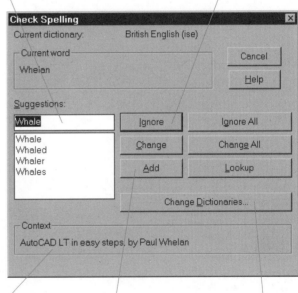

The spell check dialog box appears only if a misspelling is present in the text you select.

The sentence you select on the drawing displays here

Click here to add the word to the dictionary to be recognised the next time

Offers American and British dictionaries

Editing Text

Command line: ddedit, or the alias 'ed'

Menu: Modify > Object > Text...

Icon:

The Text command allows the editing of: a single line, paragraph and Leader text.

If the text you select is created using the Single Line Text command (dtext), its text editor appears. Simple editing can then be carried out.

The Multiline Text Editor opens only if the selected text was originally inserted using the Paragraph Text command.

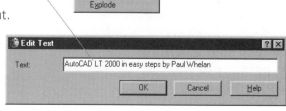

If the text you select was created by the Paragraph Text command (mtext), the Multiline Text Editor opens showing the selected text. This text can be modified: e.g. changing font, style...

The selected text is preloaded into the editor

Text Size and Plotting/Printing

When you select text height for a drawing, keep in mind the scale at which the drawing will eventually be plotted.

 If you are unsure at what scale the drawing is to be printed, input the text as though the plot is to be 1:100. Changing the text size to 1:25, or 1:250 is then easy.

Because text is often the only object on a drawing that does not represent something in the real world, it is not placed on the drawing in real-world size.

Text size on a plotted drawing

To discover the size text will be on a printed drawing, divide the text height by the plot scale. For example:

Text height input   =   500mm

Drawing plotted   =   1:100

Therefore, the text height on the plotted drawing in this example is 500/100 = 5mm.

 The phrase 'plot scale' is the scale at which the drawing is printed. If you print at 1:50, then 50 is the plot scale.

And vice versa if the text must be 8mm high on a drawing at 1:250, the calculation is:

8*250   =   2000mm

Here are some other examples:

- 4mm text is input as 400mm on a 1:100 plot

- 5mm text is input as 250mm on a 1:50 plot

- 6mm text is input as 150mm on a 1:25 plot

Multiply the height you want the text to be on the printed drawing, by the scale factor to which it is printed, to discover the text size you enter.

Text for signs on a drawing are shown in real-world size and consequently must be input in real-world size like any other object in the drawing.

Text Styles

Introduction
AutoCAD LT 2000 contains many text fonts. Each one of these fonts can be modified, by say, changing the slope angle, font 'thickness', etc. These changes constitute a style. All the fonts available in AutoCAD LT have a single predefined style known as STANDARD.

How the command works
AutoCAD LT offers you the current style. You can edit this or create an entirely new style. If you create a new style you must give it a unique name. A style can also be deleted.

Command line: ddstyle

Menu: Format > Text Style

A text style is a set of changes made to a font.

The command in action
Issue the Text Style command. Fill in the Text Style dialog box – see page 79 opposite.

This is the default AutoCAD LT style

AutoCAD LT in easy steps by Paul Whelan

The standard style modified by setting
the obliquing angle to 30 degrees

AutoCAD LT 98 in easy steps by Paul Whelan

In this style example, the standard font
was used but set running backwards

ʍɐlɘʜW lυɒԀ γd ƨqɘƚƨ γƨɒɘ ni 8Ꝑ TⳐ ᑯAϽoƚυA

Text Style Dialog Box

 The point you select to start the text on the drawing is the 'insertion point'.

To see the other fonts a style may be based on, click the down-arrow

The current style

Click New to create a new style

Allows you to rename the current style

Allows you to delete the current style

Text runs upside-down from the insertion point

Text runs backwards from the insertion point

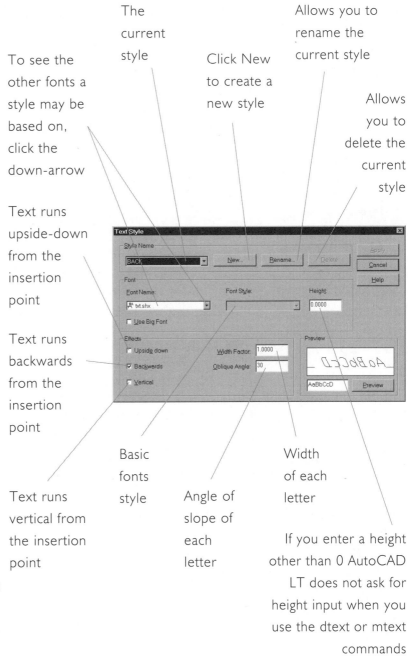

Text runs vertical from the insertion point

Basic fonts style

Angle of slope of each letter

Width of each letter

 If you enter a text height in this dialog box, the style is always set to that height.

If you enter a height other than 0 AutoCAD LT does not ask for height input when you use the dtext or mtext commands

Points

If you have layers set up for the drawing, it's a good idea to place the points on a separate layer. This allows you to make the points invisible without regenerating the complete drawing.

Introduction

A point is an object. It can be placed in the drawing as a marker to show boundaries or elevations. A point can be made invisible so that it does not plot or print. You can Object Snap to a point using the mode Node.

How the command works

Twenty basic symbols can be used to represent a point. Simply click on a position on the screen for the point.

AutoCAD LT uses the default point shape and size or the last setting used. To change these settings, see the Point Style dialog box

Command line: point, or the alias 'po'

Menu: Draw > Point > Single Point

Toolbar:

The Object Snap Node icon:

The command in action

Issue the Point command. Select the position for the point you want in the usual way. If you cannot see the point, then switch the grid off if it is displayed. If you still cannot see the point, change the Point Style.

The system variables PDMODE and PDSIZE can be used to change the size and appearance of points.

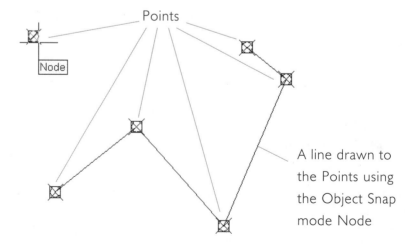

Points

Node

A line drawn to the Points using the Object Snap mode Node

Point Style

You can use only one point style at any one time.

How the command works

Select a point from the library. This then becomes the current point style. You can only use one point style at a time in a drawing.

To see the effect of selecting a new point style, you must type Regen at the command line and press Enter.

Command line: ddptype

Menu: Format > Point Style

The command in action

Issue the Point Style command. The Point Style dialog box displays. Select a point by clicking on it, then click OK.

If the drawing is very large, the Regen command may take a while to regenerate the entire drawing.

The default point is a dot

The invisible point: the points remain on the drawing but are rendered invisible

Points can be displayed as a percentage of the overall screen size

Click here to set the point size to use the units of the drawing

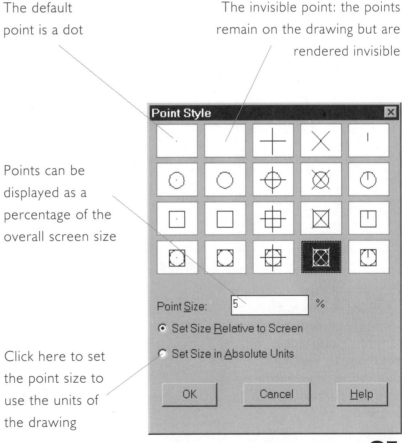

Controlling the Drawing Units

The units can be changed at any time during the drawing process.

How the command works
The Units command allows you to change the type of drawing units and their level of precision.

Command line: ddunits

Menu: Format > Units

The command in action
Issue the Units command. The Units Control dialog box displays.

Select the desired method for angle measurement here

Select the drawing units you want here

Click on the down arrow and select the level of precision you want

Only change the direction control settings to suit the discipline in which you are currently working.

Select Direction to choose the direction for zero degrees

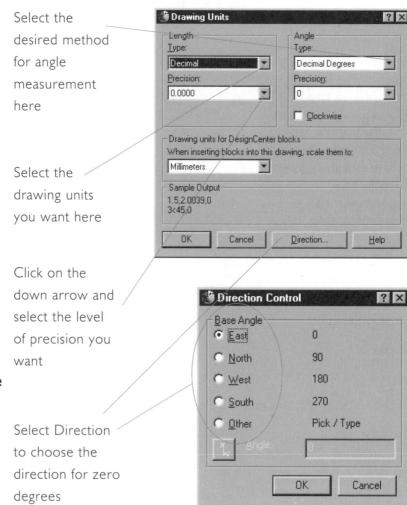

Working with Layers

In this chapter, you can learn about layers. Layers control the display of objects; they also help directly in the drawing and editing procedures by enabling you to assign colours and linetypes to them.

Covers

Chapter Seven

Layers

Introduction

An AutoCAD LT drawing can be constructed using several
layers. A layer is like a transparent sheet of paper that
holds drawing objects. For example, a drawing of the plans
of a house could be constructed as follows: the walls would
occupy a layer called 'walls', the doors and windows would
be placed on a layer called 'fittings', etc. When a drawing is
structured in this way you have control over numerous
aspects of the work.

**A layer can
be assigned
a linetype
and a
specific colour.**

AutoCAD LT supplies you with one default layer named 'o'.
Any other layers must be created by you, the user, although
you can assign as many layers as you like to a drawing. A
layer is not limited by the number of objects it can hold.
Each layer must also have its own unique name.

Layers always lie directly above or below each other and
cannot be moved. Layers can be made visible or invisible,
and can be assigned a colour or a linetype so that each
object drawn on the layer appears in the specified colour
and linetype.

Often the colour of a linetype is used to indicate the
thickness of a line. Even if the printer/plotter device you
use is monochrome, assigning colours to layers can be very
important.

This drawing is spread
over four layers

Main structure of the drawing
is placed on this layer

**If you draw
something
on the
wrong
layer, AutoCAD LT
allows you to move
an object to the
correct layer.**

Setting up a New Layer

Give layers names that describe what they contain.

Here, we will set up two layers called Walls and Fittings. To create a new layer, first issue the Layer command:

Command line: layer, or the alias 'la'

Menu: Format > Layer

Icon:

In the Layer & Linetype Properties dialog box, click on New.

The current layer – the one in which you are working – is shown as 0 here

Holds the names of all the layers set up for this drawing

Displays the linetype in use by a layer

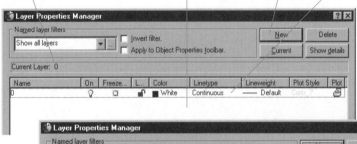

There is a special relationship between Blocks and layers (see Chapter 8).

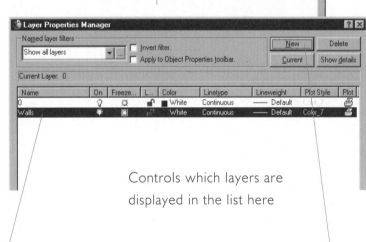

Controls which layers are displayed in the list here

You can rename a layer by highlighting its name and pressing the F2 function key.

2 Type in your Layer I named Walls and press Enter.

3 Click on New again, type in the layer name 'Fittings' and press Enter. Both layers are now set up.

Assigning a Colour to a Layer

Assigning a colour to a layer means that everything drawn on the relevant layer takes on that colour.

1 In the Layer & Linetype Properties dialog box, click on the Colour box for the 'Walls' layer.

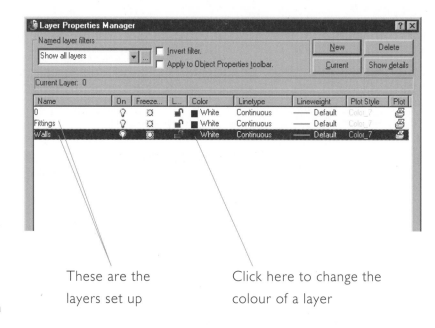

These are the
layers set up

Click here to change the
colour of a layer

To assign the same colour to several layers at once, hold down the Ctrl key and click on the name of each layer to highlight all the layers. Then click on the colour. This action opens the Select Color dialog box.

2 In the Select Color dialog box, click on the colour red for the 'Walls' layer. Then click OK.

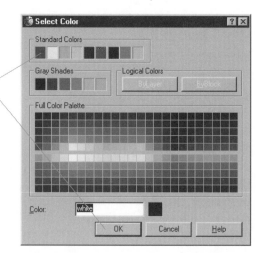

3 Assign the colour green to the layer 'Fittings'.

Making a Layer Current

A layer must be current before you can draw on it. To make the layer 'Walls' current, carry out the following easy steps:

1 Click on the layer name in the Layer & Linetype Properties dialog box, then click on the Current button.

2 Click OK to return to the drawing editor.

3 The Object Properties toolbar at the top of the screen (see below) shows the name of the current layer and its colour. Try drawing something. It appears in red.

Layers icon   Current layer and colour

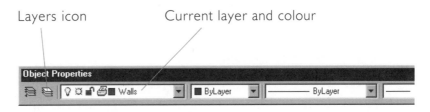

Alternatively, to make a layer current from within the drawing editor:

To follow these examples set up two layers: a 'Walls' layer with the colour red and a 'Fittings' layer in green.

1 Click here.

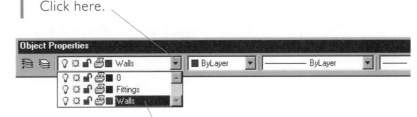

2 Click here near the layer name.

3 Click anywhere outside of the drawing editor.

Draw an object such as a line or circle and it takes on the colour property of the selected layer.

Now make the 'Fittings' layer current and draw an object on it. The drawn object should appear in green.

Making Layers Visible or Invisible

Why control the visibility of layers?

AutoCAD LT allows you to switch a layer 'off' (invisible) or 'on' (visible).

An invisible layer is not printable. **Sensitive information on a drawing can therefore be placed on a separate layer and made invisible.**

Complex drawings may become cluttered, making object selection for drawing and editing difficult. Object clutter may be reduced by making a layer invisible if you are not working on it. When a layer is made invisible, the objects drawn on it disappear from the screen, even thought they still exist and are part of the drawing. Invisible layers don't print, allowing you to print selected layers of a drawing.

For example, a builder of a house may not be interested in the furnishings which an interior designer has placed on the drawing. The furnishings layer can be made invisible and the drawing then plotted for the builder.

Several layers can be made invisible if required. The icon signalling a visible layer is a glowing light bulb. Invisibility is shown by a dull light bulb. To make a layer visible or invisible, perform the following steps:

A yellow light bulb signals that a layer is 'On' or is visible.

1 Click here.

2 Click here on the light bulb.

3 Click anywhere outside of the drawing editor.

Do not switch off the current layer. If you do, you won't be able to see what your working on.

Generally, there is no sense in making the layer you are working on (the current layer) invisible. If you attempt to switch it off, AutoCAD LT warns you.

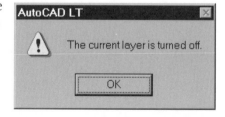

Freezing and Thawing Layers

A frozen layer cannot be made the current layer.

When a drawing is regenerated (using the Regen command) AutoCAD LT reconstructs the complete drawing from scratch. This may take a considerable length of time on a complex drawing. To save regeneration time you can freeze a layer. A frozen layer is not regenerated. Text is slow to regenerate, so you could place the text on a separate layer and freeze it.

To return a frozen layer to its normal condition you thaw it. A thawed layer is visible and does regenerate.

To freeze a layer

You can change the properties of several layers at the one time by just clicking on them.

1 Click here.

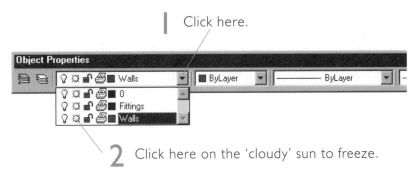

2 Click here on the 'cloudy' sun to freeze.

3 Click anywhere outside of the drawing editor.

A frozen layer is also automatically rendered invisible.

To thaw a layer

1 Click here.

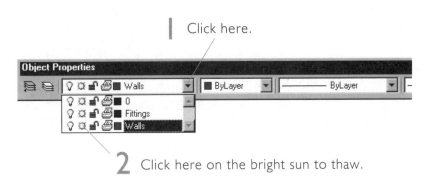

2 Click here on the bright sun to thaw.

3 Click anywhere outside of the drawing editor.

Freezing and Viewports

Freeze layers which you will not be using for a long time, and/or which contain a lot of text or hatching.

Open the Layer Properties Manager dialog box (Format > Layer command sequence). One of the column headings in the dialog box begins with: 'F...'. Pull this back to reveal the full heading by following the steps:

1 Move the cursor to here. It turns to a vertical bar with opposite-pointing arrows.

A viewport is a window set up within AutoCAD LT to allow two or more views of the same drawing (see page 180 for more on *Viewports*).

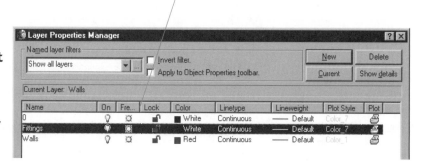

2 Hold down the left mouse button and drag to the right.

3 The full heading then becomes visible.

When you thaw a layer it regenerates, so it may take some extra time.

This refers to tiled viewports in model space

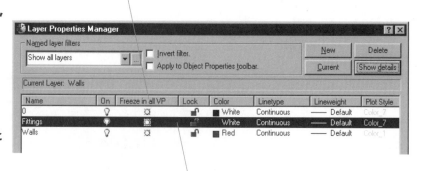

When you are using the default drawing editor, you are working in a single tiled viewport in model space.

This is useful if you are working in floating viewports. As you create new viewports the selected layers are automatically frozen

Lock, Delete and Details

Lock/Unlock

A layer can be locked. A locked layer cannot be edited, but objects on a locked layer may be used to help edit an unlocked layer. For example, you can trim a line on an unlocked layer back to a line on a locked layer. However, you cannot trim the line on the locked layer.

How to lock/unlock a layer

Lock a layer if someone else is working on the drawing and you want to 'remind' them not to change anything on that particular layer.

| Click here.

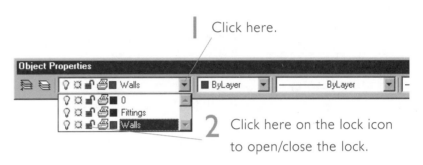

2 Click here on the lock icon to open/close the lock.

3 Click anywhere outside of the drawing editor.

If you're working with a team using a standard set of layers, don't delete any layers unless you talk to the project manager first.

Delete

A layer may be deleted if it is unreferenced. Basically this means that there must be no objects placed on it; it cannot be the default layer o; it cannot be the 'defpoints' layer (created by AutoCAD LT when you start dimensioning objects); and it cannot be part of a Block or an xref.

Details

This button provides a summary (not further details) of the selected layer.

Linetypes

Introduction

The default linetype in AutoCAD LT is continuous. Everything you draw is shown with a continuous linetype. To draw with a dashed, dotted, or other linetype you need to look in the two libraries of linetypes supplied. The libraries are found in the files *aclt.lin* and *acltiso.lin*.

If the template drawing you use is based on the acltiso template, use the acltiso.lin library.

How to access a linetype

The steps for using a linetype are: firstly the linetype must be loaded into AutoCAD LT from a library; secondly it must be set to 'current' status.

How to use a linetype

Once a linetype is loaded into AutoCAD LT, you are ready to use it by making it current. That can be done in one of the following ways:

- Assign it to a layer – this is called the Bylayer method

- Assign it to a Block – this is called the Byblock method

- Assign it to an object – to do this you just make the linetype current and draw

If you know how to set up your own template drawings, why not load all the linetypes you frequently use into the template so that they are easily available.

Linetype name   Visual description

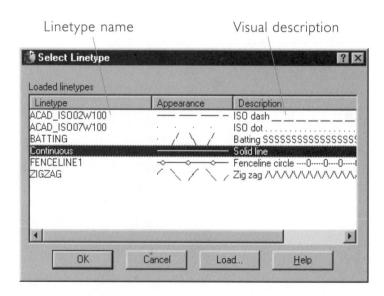

How to Load a Linetype

A linetype has to be loaded before it can be used in AutoCAD LT.

1 Under the Format menu, pick Linetype or type Linetype at the command line.

2 Click on Load.

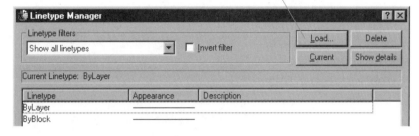

You can create your own linetypes if there are none suitable in the aclt or acltiso libraries.

3 Make sure acltiso.lin is in this box – click on File if it's missing and select it from the library list.

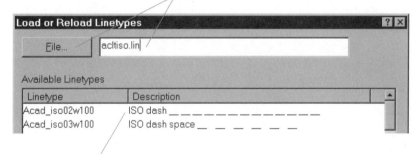

A linetype only has to be loaded once during the time you work on a file. It is saved with the file and is available the next time you open the drawing.

4 Click on the linetype you want to load – try ISO dash.

5 Click on OK.

6 The linetype is now loaded and added to the list in the Layer & Linetype Properties dialog box.

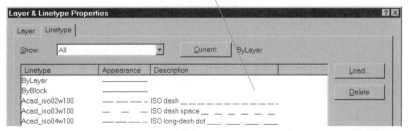

Linetypes – ßyLayer

Linetypes and layers – ßyLayer

You can associate a linetype with a layer so that the linetype automatically becomes current when the layer is current. To do this. follow the steps:

If the LTScale setting is not correct, the linetype may still look continuous.

1 Open the Layer Properties Manager dialog box by clicking on the icon 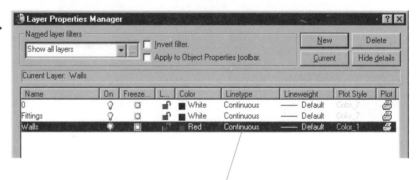 or use the Format > Layers command.

There are several other ways to carry out the procedures here. You may discover a more suitable way.

2 In the Layer Properties Manager dialog box, under Linetype, click 'Continuous'.

3 The Select Linetype dialog box appears. Select the linetype you want and click on OK. If what you want is not listed, click Load and follow the prompts for loading a linetype.

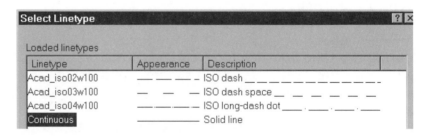

4 To see how successful you were, make the layer current and draw a line or two on it.

5 If the lines still seem continuous, see Scaling Linetypes (page 98).

Linetypes by Object

Setting a linetype current

It is possible to draw different objects on the same layer using different linetypes. To do this follow the steps below.

I   On the Object Properties toolbar pick the down arrow for linetypes. Only linetypes already loaded into AutoCAD are displayed here.

2   Select the linetype you want to use. This sets the linetype current regardless of the lintype/layer setting.

3   You should now be able to draw in the selected lintype. To return to drawing with the linetype assigned to the layer, select Bylayer in Step 1 above.

The Details linetype option

The Details Category in the Layers Properties Manager may also be used to assign a linetype to a layer.

AutoCAD LT 2000 also allows you to assign a weight to a line so that it appears in the drawing editor with a thickness.

Making a Layer Current by Object

To draw on a layer, you first need to make it current. If you have objects drawn on a layer already, and if you wish to make that layer current then use the icon: 📑

In the illustration below, the circle and the line are on different layers. The line is on the current layer, but to make the layer the circle is on current, carry out the following steps:

1 Click on the Layers icon. 📑

2 Click on the circle.

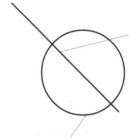

Line is on the current layer

The layer the circle is on is now
made current by selecting it

How to Unlock a Layer

1 Click on the Layers icon.

You can also lock/ unlock a layer using the Object Properties toolbar (see page 91). Try it!

2 Select the layer name you want to unlock.

3 Click on 'Details >>' at the bottom of the dialog box.

4 Remove the tick from the 'Lock or editing' box.

Moving Objects to a Different Layer

If you draw an object on the wrong layer, AutoCAD LT allows you to place the object on the correct layer without redrawing it. Each object in a drawing has properties associated with it. The colour of an object or the layer it is on are examples of properties.

To change the layer an object is on, use the Change Properties command.

How the command works
Select the object you want to move to a new layer and then select the layer you want:

Command line: ddchprop

Menu: Modify > Properties...

The command in action

The dialog box displayed at Step 2 may differ from that shown. In the illustration on this page, an xref was selected, so AutoCAD LT displayed the Modify External Reference dialog box.

1   Issue the command. The Properties box appears. Select the Categorized tab.

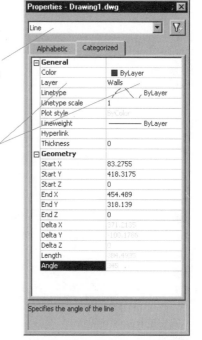

2   Select the object you want to change in the drawing editor. It highlights with Grips. In this example, a Line is selected.

3   Click on Layer, then select the layer you want from the list.

4   The line immediatly moves to the selected layer. Close the Properties box by clicking on the X icon at the top right of the box.

Scaling Linetypes – Ltscale

The scale of a linetype (or ltscale) refers to the spacing of the elements that make up the linetype. For example, the dashes in a linetype may be 4 units long and the spaces 2 units.

Examples here use the Line object, but the same explanation applies for any object drawn in a particular linetype.

These spacings can be scaled up or down from the default settings. The default setting is a scale of 1. To change the ltscale on a dashed linetype carry out the following steps:

1 From the Modify menu, select Properties.

2 The Properties dialog box displays.

3 Click on the linetype you want to readjust in the drawing editor.

4 Select Linetype Scale from the Propteries box and enter the scale you want.

5 Close the Properties box by clicking on the X icon at the top right of the box.

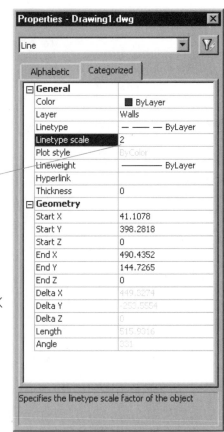

Properties - Drawing1.dwg

Line

Alphabetic | Categorized

General	
Color	■ ByLayer
Layer	Walls
Linetype	— — — ByLayer
Linetype scale	2
Plot style	ByColor
Lineweight	———— ByLayer
Hyperlink	
Thickness	0
Geometry	
Start X	41.1078
Start Y	398.2818
Start Z	0
End X	490.4352
End Y	144.7265
End Z	0
Delta X	449.3274
Delta Y	-253.5554
Delta Z	0
Length	515.9916
Angle	331

Specifies the linetype scale factor of the object

Blocks and Xrefs

Blocks are formed by grouping objects together. You will learn to insert Blocks and drawings into other drawings. The difference between Blocks and xrefs is explained, and then xrefs are treated in full. Finally, we examine how to organise Blocks and xrefs using the Design Center.

Covers

Chapter Eight

What is a Block?

 Once a Block is made, follow a special procedure to edit it. See the Explode command on page 105.

A Block is an object or group of objects gathered together and given a name. Once the group of objects has a unique name you can use it in the drawing as many times as you like. You can also use it in drawings other than the one in which it was created.

You can build up your own library of Blocks or purchase third-party libraries. Typical examples of Blocks are doors and windows, or electrical components such as switches and transistors.

A complete drawing can be treated as a Block. For example you could draw a room and later add it into a separate drawing of a house.

A Block has an insertion point. This is the point that is picked up for insertion into a drawing.

 Draw Blocks at real-world size to make the task much easier.

Three examples of Blocks

1. A Block of a door

Here, the arc and lines are grouped together and given a name. This is called a Block.

Possible insertion point

Lines

Arc

2. A Block of a man

 Keep all the Blocks you make in a separate folder from that containing your drawings.

Lines

Possible insertion point

Circle

3. A Block of a barge

Spline   Possible insertion point   Lines

Arc

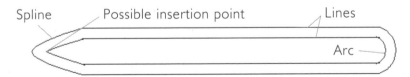

Blocks and Layers

A Block can be created on a single layer or spread over several layers. The layers on which a Block is created can affect the performance of the Blocks when used in a drawing at a later stage.

Layer O Blocks

Layer o is quite special. Any Block created on layer o positions itself on the current layer when the Block is placed in a drawing. The Block then takes on the properties of that layer.

If a Block is spread over several layers, it brings those layers into a drawing when it is inserted.

Here is an example: imagine a drawing with just two layers – layer o (white) and layer 'Walls' (red). If a Block is created wholly on layer o, it becomes white in colour.

If a user then makes layer 'Walls' (red) current and inserts the Block into the drawing, the Block 'sits' into the layer 'Walls' and now appears red in colour.

Lastly, when this Block is exploded for editing, it falls back down to layer o and takes on the properties of that layer.

Blocks created on layers other than O

If a Block is created on several layers other than layer o, the Block carries those layers and their properties around with it into whatever drawing it is inserted.

Layer O Blocks have the special property of always inserting onto the current layer when placed into a drawing.

Here is an example: imagine a Block is created from objects on two layers – Walls (red) and Windows (yellow). If this Block is inserted into a drawing that does not contain those layers, then the layers are automatically created by the Block as it is inserted.

The layers have the same properties as the original two layers – red and yellow. This action occurs even if the current layer at the time of insertion is layer o.

If this Block is exploded for editing, the objects of the Block will fall back to their original layers.

How to Make a Block

Sequence: Overall view

- Draw the objects that make up the Block.

- Give a name to the Block.

- Decide where the insertion point should be. This is important because you can insert the Block into a drawing using Object Snap.

- Group the objects together.

The example Block being created here can only be inserted into the drawing into which it was created.

Follow these easy steps:

1 Draw the door.

2 Click on Draw.

3 Click on Block.

4 Click on Make.

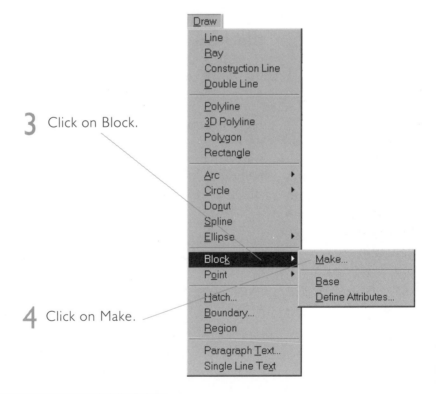

50mm

900mm

Arc

...cont'd

5 The following dialog box appears.

6 Type 'Door1'.

7 Click to place a dot here.

8 Click here and then pick an insertion point on the drawing of the door. Use Object Snap.

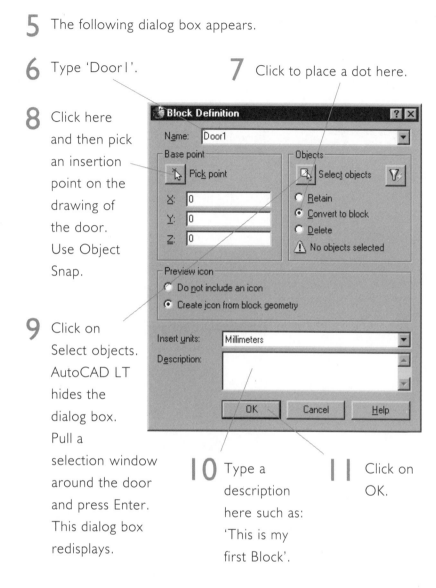

Block Definition

Name: Door1

Base point
Pick point
X: 0
Y: 0
Z: 0

Objects
Select objects
○ Retain
● Convert to block
○ Delete
⚠ No objects selected

Preview icon
○ Do not include an icon
● Create icon from block geometry

Insert units: Millimeters

Description:

OK   Cancel   Help

9 Click on Select objects. AutoCAD LT hides the dialog box. Pull a selection window around the door and press Enter. This dialog box redisplays.

10 Type a description here such as: 'This is my first Block'.

11 Click on OK.

If an error message tells you the Block name is incorrect, try removing spaces from the name.

How to Insert a Block

This Block can only be inserted into the drawing in which it was created.

Once the Block has been created, you may insert it into the drawing. Try this now using the Block 'Door1':

1 Click on the Insert menu.

2 Click on the Block... command.

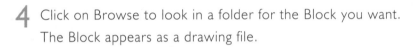

3 The Insert dialog box then appears.

4 Click on Browse to look in a folder for the Block you want. The Block appears as a drawing file.

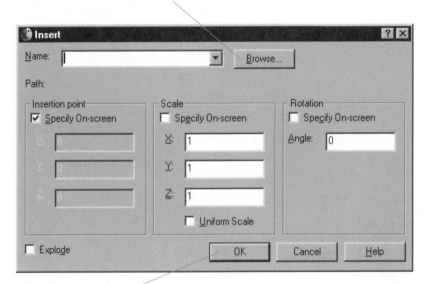

5 Click OK.

6 At this stage, AutoCAD LT returns you to the drawing with the Block attached to the crosshairs at the insertion point you defined.

...cont'd

Step 8: if you move the cursor at this Step, you will see the effect of scaling on the X and Y axis.

7 Move the Block into position on the screen. The command line asks for an Insertion point. Click on a point on the drawing to show where you want to place the Block.

8 AutoCAD LT now needs to know if you would like to scale the Block on the X axis. Press Enter to accept the default value of 1 (for no scaling).

There is a close relation-ship between Blocks and layers. Make sure you understand layers before you create a library of Blocks.

9 AutoCAD LT next needs to know if you would like to scale the Block on the Y axis. Press Enter to accept the default value of 1 (for no scaling).

10 The command line needs to know if you would like to rotate the Block. You could type in an angle and press Enter or just press Enter to accept the default of 0.

11 The Block is now locked into position in the drawing.

If you don't have enough time to master layers before working on Blocks, make sure that you use the default layer 0 when creating your Blocks.

This Block behaves as a single object when you try to edit it. You can demonstrate this for yourself.

For example: try the Move command on it: the moment you select it, the Block appears as a single entity.

Exploding a Block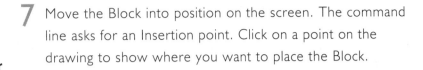

To edit or change some detail within a Block you first need to 'explode' the Block.

Any modifications made to the exploded Block do not affect the original Block you defined.

Placing One Drawing into Another

Any AutoCAD LT drawing can be placed into another AutoCAD LT drawing. In the Block Insert dialog box, select File instead of Block.

The inserted drawing behaves like a Block.

Insert only a finished drawing, otherwise you will have to explode it for editing. This could cause problems unless you are highly skilled with AutoCAD LT.

1 Click on the Insert menu.

2 Click on the Block... command.

Insert
Block...
External Reference...
Layout ▶
Windows Metafile...
OLE Object...
Xref Manager...
Hyperlink...   Ctrl+K

3 The Insert dialog box appears.

Insert   ? ✕

Name: [▼]   [Browse...]

Path:

4 Click on Browse.

5 Select Drawing File dialog box and look for the file you want.

Visual preview of the highlighted drawing

Select Drawing File   ? ✕

Look in: AutoCAD LT 2000

- Drv
- Fonts
- Help
- Plot Styles
- Plotters
- Sample
- Support
- Template
- a_pip.dwg

Preview

File name: a_pip.dwg   [Open]

Files of type: Drawing (*.dwg)   [Cancel]

Find File...

Locate

6 Click on Open when you have found the desired file. This action returns you to the Insert dialog box. The path to the drawing file is now shown in the box.

...cont'd

If you cannot find the file you want, you may need to develop your skill in searching folders. See 'Windows 95/ 98/2000 in easy steps'.

7 Click OK to proceed with the insertion of the file. All files have a base point of 0,0 (attached to the cross-hairs).

8 Pick an insertion point (or type a co-ordinate).

9 AutoCAD LT now asks questions about scaling on the X and Y axis and the rotation angle. Complete these as requested.

How to Change the Base Point

The default base point for a drawing is 0,0. To change the base point, perform the following steps:

1 Open the drawing.

2 Click on the Draw menu. Select Block and then click on Base.

If you insert a drawing and you cannot see its entire extent, try typing Z for zoom and pressing Enter, and then E for extents followed by Enter.

3 AutoCAD LT asks you to pick a new base point. Use Object Snap or an absolute co-ordinate if you wish.

```
Draw
  Line
  Ray
  Construction Line
  Double Line

  Polyline
  3D Polyline
  Polygon
  Rectangle

  Arc          ▶
  Circle       ▶
  Donut
  Spline
  Ellipse      ▶

  Block        ▶      Make...
  Point        ▶
                     Base
  Hatch...            Define Attributes...
  Boundary...
  Region
```

When you insert the drawing file AutoCAD LT attaches it to the cross-hairs at this point.

How to Use a Block in any Drawing

Blocks created in AutoCAD LT 2000 do not need to have this procedure carried out.

In releases of AutoCAD LT previous to LT 2000, you had to specify that you wanted to use a Block in a drawing other than the one in which it was defined. The example on this page is for AutoCAD LT 98. If a Block is converted into a drawing file then you can use it in any other drawing created by AutoCAD LT.

1 Click on Block from the Draw drop-down menu.

2 Click on Make from the cascading menu.

3 Click on the DWG file Option button.

4 Type in a name for the Block.

The Browse button can help find a folder

If a Block was originally created as an internal Block, carry out the same procedure again with the dot placed in DWG file Option button (Step 3).

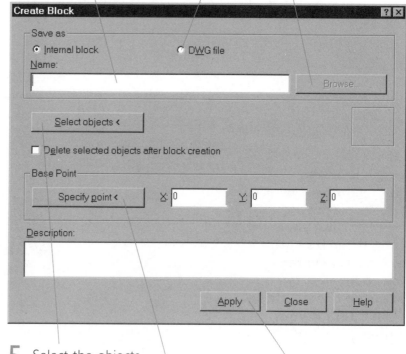

5 Select the objects.

6 Specify the insertion point.

7 Click on Apply.

External References – Xrefs

External references (or xrefs) allow you to link two or more drawings together. Below are three separate drawings:

Separate drawing file of a ball

Separate drawing file of a chair

Separate drawing file of a table

 An xref is very different from a Block. A Block becomes part of the drawing into which it is inserted; an external referenced file does not.

The drawing of the table could make reference to the ball and chair drawings to produce the following drawing.

In this example the table is the *master* drawing that makes reference to two external drawings – the chair and the ball. The ball and chair drawings are not inserted into the master drawing of the table (as a Block could be), but instead are *attached* to the table drawing. The Xref command allows you to attach drawings to a master drawing.

 A drawing that references other drawings is called the 'master' file in AutoCAD LT.

If the drawing file of the chair is changed in any way, then the chair in the master drawing also changes. This is better than if the chair was inserted as a Block, because if the Block drawing was changed, then the change would not be seen in the master drawing.

A Block becomes part of the drawing into which it is inserted. Whereas an external reference always remains a separate drawing.

How to Use Xrefs

To follow this section on xrefs you should create three simple drawings – of the chair, table and ball – and name them accordingly.

The ball is a simple circle while the table and chair are constructed from lines. Create each of the images on a sheet of 420mm by 297mm.

Once you have done this, open the drawing of the table. Then attach the drawing of the ball by creating an xref to it.

Attaching the Xref files – ball and chair

Issue the Xref command by either typing xref at the command line and pressing Enter or from the Insert toolbar select 🔲. The drop-down menu option is shown here:

| Select External Reference...

2 Click on Attach to proceed.

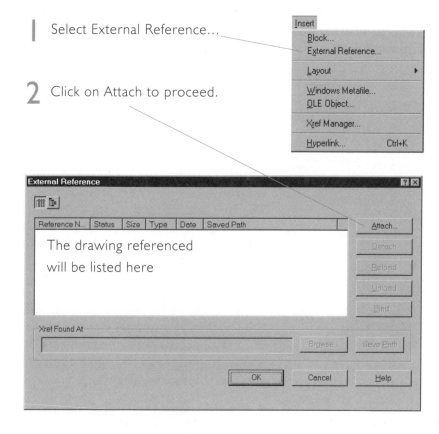

...cont'd

3 From the Select Reference File dialog box, highlight the file
you want. Check the Preview to see a sample. Then click
Open.

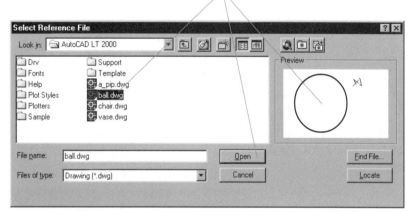

Make sure the dot is
present here

You may scale the drawing. In this
example leave it unscaled (that is 1)

 **Keep the
names of
files used
in xrefs as
short as possible.**

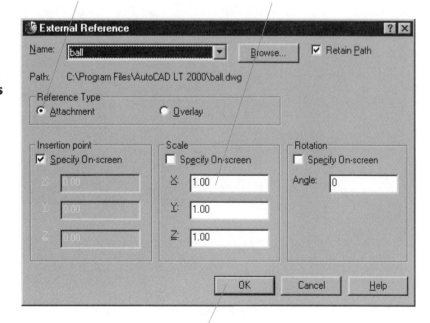

4 Confirm your selection in the Attach Xref External Reference
dialog box. Then click OK to continue.

...cont'd

5 The drawing appears attached to the cross-hairs. Position it on the table.

6 Issue the External Reference command again.

An xref file is not part of the drawing to which it is attached.

7 Click on Attach in the dialog box.

8 Click on Browse.

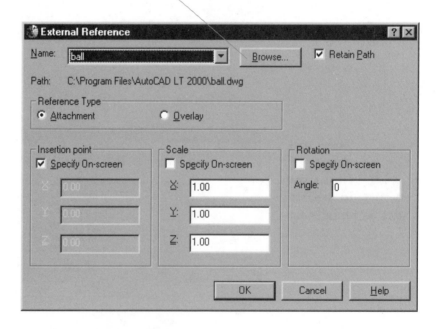

9 Select the Chair file and click on Open, and then on OK and position the chair in the drawing.

10 The files are attached. Save the drawing.

The Value of Xrefs

The value of xrefs are now illustrated below:

An xref updates auto-matically in the drawing to which it is attached.

1 Open the drawing of the chair and edit it so that it looks like this.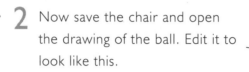

2 Now save the chair and open the drawing of the ball. Edit it to look like this.

3 Save the ball drawing and open the table drawing. It should look like this.

A Block becomes part of the drawing into which it is inserted. Blocks do not update when modified.

The edits to the attached drawing are reflected in the master drawing. This occurs because the xrefs are not saved with the table drawing. Only the link to the attachments is saved.

Each time the master drawing of the table is open AutoCAD LT checks the contents of the attached drawings: any changes made to them are automatically displayed.

A drawing can have any number of xrefs.

The value of this can be seen on large projects. A master drawing can contain references to other drawings. Each of the attached drawings can be as complex as you like and can be created by different individuals on a network. As work proceeds, the master drawing always shows the latest state of the drawings.

Working with Xrefs

A drawing containing an external reference must always have access to the referenced drawing while it is attached. This means that you cannot move the master drawing or the xrefs to another folder.

Try and keep the master drawing and its xrefs in the same folder.

The illustration below shows four folders: folder 1 contains the master drawing with xrefs in folders 2, 3 and 4. If the xref in folder 2 is moved to folder 3, the master drawing will not be able to find it.

A master drawing always looks for its external references each time the drawing is opened.

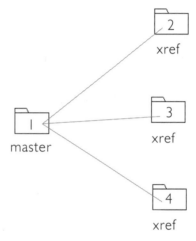

This can lead to problems if a large number of xrefs are being used. A good tip for this kind of work is to keep the master drawing and all its external references in one folder.

It is then easy to move the master drawing and its xrefs, particularly if you want to send the drawing to someone else to complete.

Do not move the location of an xref. If you do, the master drawing will not be able to find it.

When a project is finished you can bind the xrefs into the master drawing so that they behave like Blocks: they become part of the drawing and do not update automatically. The master drawing does not then look for them again.

Detaching an Xref

You may decide that an xref is no longer required in a drawing. Using the Erase command does not remove the xref: it will erase the image on the screen but when you open the master drawing again the xref reappears.

To remove any reference to the xref you must *detach* it as follows:

You must detach an xref if you want to remove it from the drawing.

1 From the Insert menu click on Xref Manager.

2 In the Xref Manager dialog box, highlight the xref you want to detach.

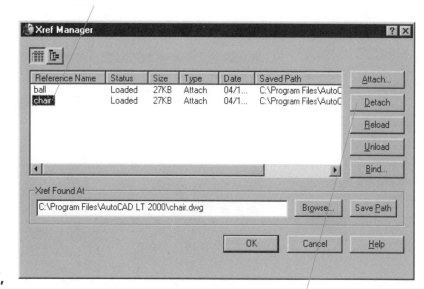

If you use the Erase command on an xref, it reappears in the drawing the next time you open it.

3 Click on Detach and click OK to return to the drawing. The xref you choose is removed.

You must Attach the drawing file again if you want to use it as an xref.

Binding an Xref

Once a drawing is finished you might like to bind the external references into the master drawing. This action ensures that the master drawing does not look for the xrefs again. The xrefs become part of the drawing and are stored as part of the master drawing file. This allows you to send the finished drawing to other people. To bind the chair created on pages 109–110, follow the steps below.

A bound xref is not updated.

1 Open the master drawing. Click on Insert > Xref Manager.

2 The Xref Manager dialog box lists the drawings already attached to the master drawing. Select the file you want to bind by highlighting it, then click on Bind.

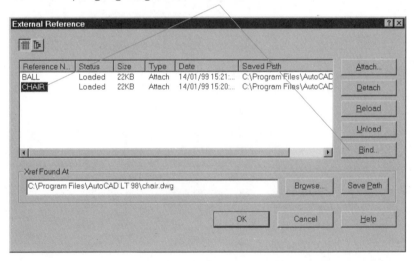

3 Two options are presented in the Bind Xrefs box: Bind and Insert.

Keeps the xref image in the drawing with separate layers

Keeps an xref as if it were inserted as a Block, and so merging it with the master drawing

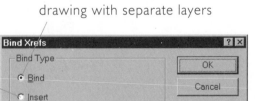

Other Xref Options

Unload

The Unload command prevents the xref from being displayed on the screen, although it still remains attached to the drawing. You might Unload if the drawing screen is cluttered and the xref is not needed at the time of editing.

Reload

The Reload command forces AutoCAD LT to re-display an xref again. This can be used if the Unload command was applied or if you want to check if a referenced drawing has changed since you opened the master.

Know the locations of xrefs in a drawing if you unload them, otherwise you may draw something in the positions they occupy.

List View   Tree View   Click a heading to sort a list

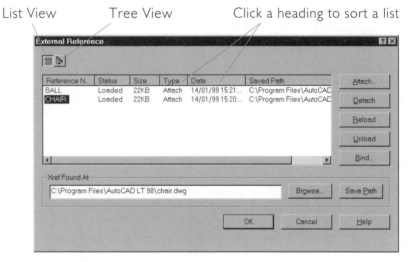

On a project that involves the use of xrefs, it should be agreed about the location of all xrefs and the layering system in use.

Save Path

The Save Path command saves the path to the folder containing the referenced file. If the xref is moved, you can use Browse and reset the path in this way.

List View

The List View command simply lists the attached files. Clicking on the headings Size, Type, etc, sorts the files under the selected heading.

Tree View

The Tree View command provides more detailed information about the xrefs than is available in List View.

Xrefs and the List Command

The terms xref and external reference have the same meaning.

You can use the List command to check information about any object in a drawing. Type List at the command line and click on the xrefs in the master drawing.

In the example below, the ball and chair are selected. Both are externally referenced drawings. The List command is especially useful if you have to look at someone else's drawing and it can be applied to any AutoCAD LT object.

The chair is still an xref

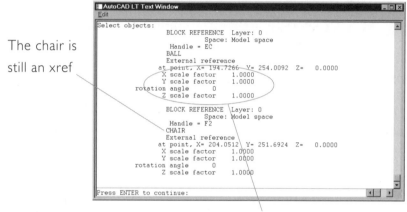

A scale factor of 1 means the drawing was referenced as it was drawn (i.e. no scaling)

The List command provides information on all xrefs that a drawing contains, if you input '-xref' at the command line and use the '?' option

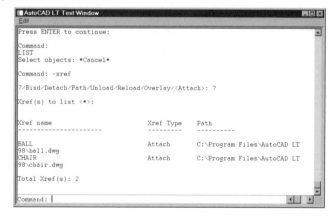

Design Center

The Design Center is AutoCAD LT's own file manager. It can help you:

- View the Blocks and xrefs in a drawing file

- Insert Blocks and xrefs by dragging them into the drawing

- Copy drawings and Blocks from one folder to another

- Group together files needed for the same project

- Search for files on the disk or network

The Design Center is found under the Tools drop-down menu. When this is opened, the default display shows the Blocks present in the current drawing.

Tree view
toggle option

Icon used to
search for
files

Icon
representing the
current drawing

Pick on Blocks to see
which Blocks are in
this drawing

In this example,
the drawing has
a Block of a car
inserted

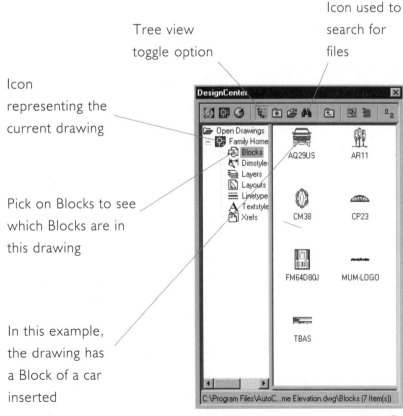

What the Design Center Shows You

AutoCAD LT drawings can be seen as a database. As work on a drawing progresses, all the objects drawn on the screen are placed into this databse.

The Design Center allows you to look at the database and copy elements from it into another drawing. Note the following about the use of the Design Center.

- When you select a folder, the drawings it contains are displayed as icons

- If you pick on a drawing icon in the Tree view the Blocks, Layers, Dimstyles, Layouts (of Paper Space), Linetypes, Textstyles and Xrefs are displayed

- If you pick on the plus sign in front of the drawing name, a tree view of the above elements is shown

- If you select one of these elements, for example, Blocks, you can see a list of the Blocks in the drawing

 The Design Center allows you to take elements from one drawing to another. This allows companies to produce drawings that have a consistent style.

Tree view of the elements in a drawing

Picking on the minus sign closes the tree view of the elements in a drawing

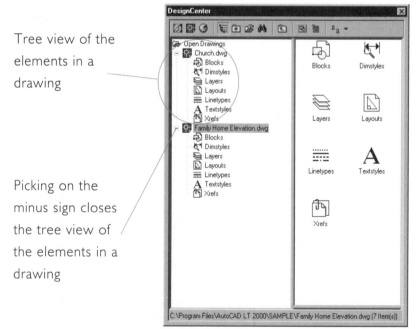

Inserting Blocks

The Design Center allows you to insert Blocks, hatch patterns, dimension styles, etc., simply by dragging the components into the current drawing.

Because all drawing in AutoCAD is done at scale 1:1 (including Blocks) a Block inserts at the correct scale. Try the following:

AutoCAD LT 2000 allows you to use the Design Center to place hatching in a drawing. See Chapter 13 for more information about hatching.

1 Open an existing drawing or start up a new one. In this example, we opened a sample drawing called 'Family Home Elevation'.

2 Open the Design Center (Tools > Design Center). Pick on 'drawing name' in the tree view, then pick on Blocks. This enables you to see which Blocks are already present in the drawing.

3 Drag one of the symbols, such as a car, over to the current drawing.

4 A Block is placed in the drawing where you drop it. The Block can be inserted repeatedly from the library.

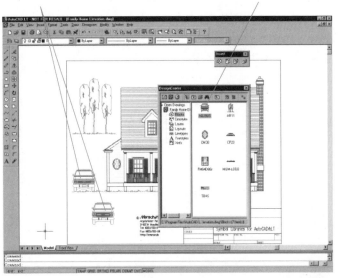

Copying a Dimension Style

The Design Center allows you to take a dimension style you create in one drawing (see page 145) and copy/transfer it to another drawing.

To do this you need to open the Design Center in Tree view. Then perform the steps below:

Dimension styles provide consistency to a drawing. A company can produce drawings with consistent styles by copying a style from one drawing to another.

1 Open the drawing into which you want to place the desired dimension style.

2 Pick the Desktop icon and look for the drawing with the dimension style you want.

3 Pick the Dimstyles icon in the drawing. Select the style and draw it into the current drawing.

4 Check the Dimstyles in the current drawing. You then see the new style added.

Several styles can be copied to a drawing providing even more scope for greater consistency.

The Desktop icon

Select the dimension style you want and draw it into the current drawing

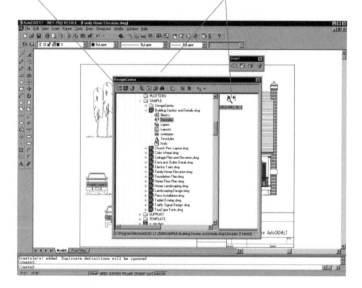

Searching using the Design Center

The Design Center allows you to search for drawings, Blocks, hatch patterns, dimension styles, linetypes etc., using the Search tool.

In this example we'll search for a dimension style called 'Exterior'.

1 Start the Design Center.

2 Pick on the Search icon.

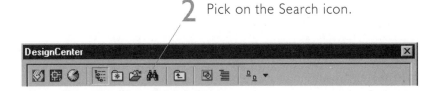

3 The Find dialog box displays.

4 Pick here to see a list of the drawing items for which you can search. Select the Dimstyles item.

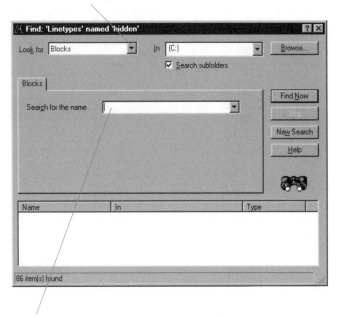

5 Type the name of the dimension style you want in here.

6 Click the Browse button and select the drive or folder in which you want to search. Place a tick in the Search sub-folders you want.

7 Pick on the Search icon.

8 A result is displayed as shown below. To use a found style simply drag it into the current drawing.

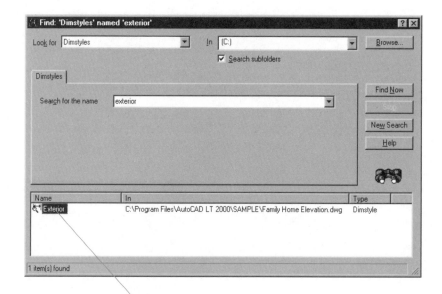

Drag the dimension style you want into the current drawing

Dimensioning

The primary function of a Computer Aided Design drawing is to supply enough information about an object to enable its construction. Dimensioning is an essential visual guide to help someone interpret the drawing for construction. AutoCAD LT 2000 has many tools for dimensioning drawings, positioning dimensions and later editing them. In this chapter, we introduce many of these dimensioning tools and the techniques for using them.

Covers

Chapter Nine

Dimensioning Overview

AutoCAD LT has many tools to help you to place dimensions on a drawing. There is no need to draw dimension lines or calculate a dimension value: AutoCAD LT does this for you.

Some of the terms used in relation to dimensioning are illustrated below.

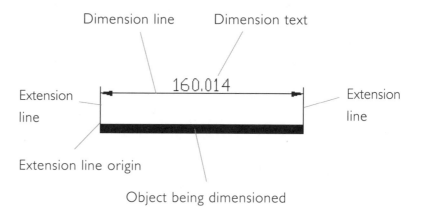

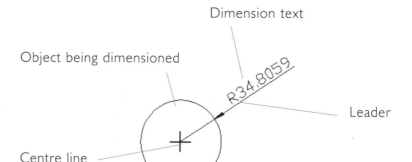

Associative dimensioning

Associative dimensioning associates a dimension with an object. When the object being dimensioned is changed in any way, that change is shown immediately in the dimension, so there is no need to re-dimension an object that has already been dimensioned. Associative dimensioning can be switched off if desired.

The Dimensioning Toolbar

Call up using the View drop-down menu: View > Toolbars, and place a tick opposite Dimension in the list of toolbars.

Dimension Update: allows individual elements of a dimension to be updated

Current Dimension Style

Dimension Style: enables creation of styles for dimensioning in engineering, architectural drawing, etc.

Dimension Text Edit: for editing dimension text

Dimension Edit: to reposition dimension text

Center Mark: places centre marks on circles & arcs

Tolerance: to insert geometric tolerances

Leader Line: used for annotations

Continue dimension: allows contiguous dimensions to aligned

Baseline Dimension: allows dimensions to be measured from a datum line and stacked at a specified distance

Angular Dimension: dimensions the angular distance between two objects

Diameter Dimension: places a diameter dimension on circles

Radius Dimension: places a radius dimension on circles and arcs

Ordinate (datum) Dimensions: measure a perpendicular distance from an origin

Aligned Dimension: dimensions lines that are not horizontal or vertical

Linear Dimension: dimensions horizontal and vertical lines

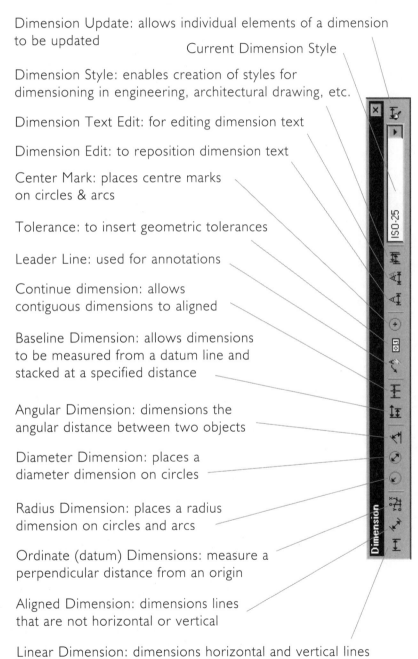

Linear Dimensioning

To dimension an object (it can be horizontal or vertical) follow the steps below. In this example the dimension is applied to a horizontal polyline.

1   Click on the Linear dimension icon. AutoCAD LT responds with 'Specify first extension line origin or <select object>.

2   Press the Enter key or the right mouse button and AutoCAD LT responds: 'Select object to dimension'.

3   Select the polyline by picking on it. AutoCAD LT immediately calculates the length of the object and now asks: 'Specify dimension line location?' or [mtext/Text/Angle/Horizontal/Vertical/Rotated].

 Read the command line carefully throughout the dimensioning procedure.

4   To position the dimension line, move the cursor above or below the polyline and pick a point. The dimension is now locked into position.

Unhappy with how the dimension looks?

Dimension text may look too small or too big, the arrows may be the wrong size, or perhaps the extension lines may run too close to the polyline. All these features can be individually modified to form a dimensioning style (see page 144).

For now, let's change all the above elements by scaling them up. The setting for the size of all the dimension elements is held in a system variable (see page 40) called DIMSCALE. By changing the dimscale value you affect the display of the dimension. Try the following:

1   Type DIMSCALE at the command line and press Enter. The response may be 'New value for DIMSCALE <1.0000>:'.

2   Type in a value greater than the default value. In this example, try 2, and press Enter.

3 AutoCAD LT returns you to a blank line prompt. Nothing appears to have happened. You now need to update the dimension to see the new setting take effect. Click on the Dimension Update icon .

4 Select the dimension. Selection is made by picking anywhere on the dimension (text or lines). The dimension is highlighted. Press Enter.

5 All aspects of the dimension increase in size – the arrows, the text, etc.

The dimensioned polyline with DIMSCALE set to I

160.014

The dimensioned polyline shown below when the Update Dimension is applied after the DIMSCALE value is set to 3.

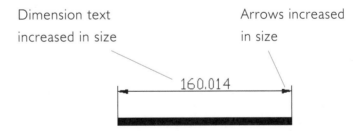

Dimension text
increased in size

Arrows increased
in size

160.014

Dimscale affects the setting in the leader lines. Dimscale does not affect the actual length of a dimension or the object being dimensioned.

Object Snap and Dimensioning

You can use the Object Snap tools to tell AutoCAD LT the position of the extension lines. This is useful if you are dimensioning across several different lines.

Consider the example below in which a line and a polyline run end to end. The linear dimension must measure from one end of the line to the other end of the polyline.

Left ▬▬▬▬▬▬▬▬▬▬▬ ————————— Right

Polyline   Line

You can just as easily use the Object Snap toolbar instead of using the Shift and right-click combination.

| Select the Linear Dimension icon. In response to: 'Specify first extension line origin' hold the Shift key down, right-click the mouse and select Endpoint from the menu.

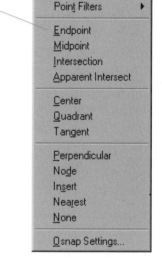

```
Tracking
From
Point Filters          ▶

Endpoint
Midpoint
Intersection
Apparent Intersect

Center
Quadrant
Tangent

Perpendicular
Node
Insert
Nearest
None

Osnap Settings...
```

2 Move the cursor to the left end of the polyline and select. AutoCAD LT now needs to know the: 'Specify the second extension line origin'. Again, hold Shift and right-click the mouse button. Select Endpoint from the menu and pick the right end of the line.

129.2001

First extension line origin selected using Object Snap Endpoint

Second extension line origin selected using Object Snap Endpoint

Ordinate Dimensioning

Introduction

Ordinate dimensions always refer back to a specific location on a drawing. In the default settings in AutoCAD LT 2000 the origin is at the bottom left of the screen. All the dimensions are based on this origin. You may set up a separate origin and mark co-ordinates on your drawing which refer to this origin.

This can ensure more accuracy in a drawing, particularly for those objects drawn that might be cut by a lathe or milling machine, or which otherwise need a high degree of accuracy.

 To switch on the Dimension toolbar click on Toolbars from the View menu.

Setting up an ordinate dimension

Draw an object or two in AutoCAD LT. We will first mark an ordinate dimension, leaving the origin at the bottom left of the screen. You can switch on the icon which shows you where the origin is by following these steps:

1 Type UCSICON at the command line and press Enter.

2 Type On and press Enter or the Spacebar.

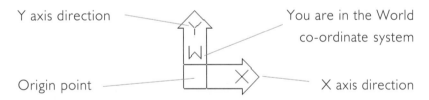

Y axis direction

You are in the World co-ordinate system

Origin point

X axis direction

Before you proceed, it's a good idea to turn Ortho on so that the leader lines from the ordinate dimension are vertical and/or horizontal.

 To switch Ortho on, just single-click on the word Ortho at the bottom of the screen.

Click on the Ordinate icon ⊞ from the Dimensions toolbar. Use Object Snap to select the endpoint of the entity. Click again to position the ordinate leader line along the X axis. Repeat the procedure for the Y axis.

Ordinate dimensions at the end of a polyline

144.232

34.778

...cont'd

In this example, the origin 0,0 is moved onto an object and an ordinate reading is then placed at another point on the same object.

The block of the chair is used in this illustration.

Moving the UCS

Hold down the Shift key and right-click to use the Object Snap modes instead of using the toolbar.

1 At the command line type UCS and press Enter. Respond to the prompt by typing M for Move and pressing Enter. AutoCAD LT then needs to know the position of the new origin. Use Object Snap to snap to the bottom left of the chair.

Step 1 places the origin here

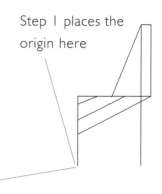

Placing the ordinate dimension

2 Click on the Ordinate icon and use Object Snap to snap to the bottom left of the chair. If you forgot to switch Ortho on, do so now. Position the X ordinate. Repeat the procedure for the Y ordinate.

3 Now place an ordinate dimension at the top right of the chair using the same procedure.

The ordinate dimension 'proves' that this is the origin

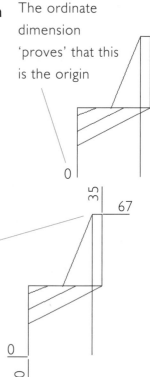

The chair with both ordinate dimensions in place

Aligned Dimensioning

The Aligned Dimension is for linear objects that are not vertical or horizontal. However, it may also be used for horizontal and vertical lines. It works the same way as the linear dimensioning on page 128.

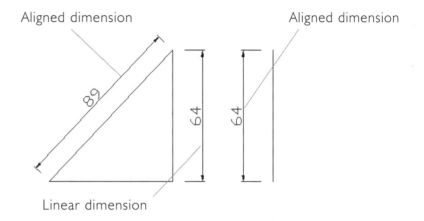

In this illustration, the vertical lines are dimensioned with the Linear and Aligned options.

Center Mark

A Center Mark shows the centre of circles, arcs and fillet arcs. When you click on the Center Mark icon ⊡ AutoCAD LT asks you to select the arc or circle you want. Once you click on the circle or arc, the Center Mark is positioned and the command ends.

The Center Mark is composed of two lines, each of which can be erased separately.

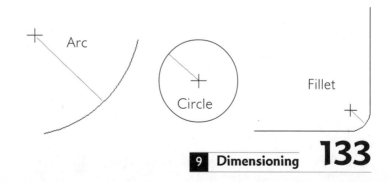

Radius and Diameter

AutoCAD LT 2000 can quickly calculate the radius and diameter of circles, arcs and fillet arcs.

In the case of a radius, AutoCAD LT places the letter 'R' for radius in front of the measurement and for diameters it places the diameter symbol.

To position a radius, click on the Radius icon and select the arc or circle.

You can move the values into position by moving the cursor. Try placing them inside and outside a circle.

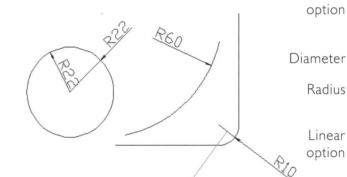

Continue option

Diameter

Radius

Linear option

AutoCAD LT draws the dimension line from the centre of the selected arc or circle automatically

To position a diameter, click on the Diameter icon and select the arc or circle.

To lock the dimensioning into vertical and horizontal positions, switch on Ortho (F8 function key) before you dimension.

You can move the values into position by moving the cursor. Try placing them inside and outside of a circle.

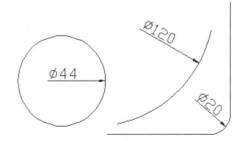

Continue Dimensioning

The Continue Dimension function allows you to run a series of linear dimensions that are always positioned at the same level. You can see an example in the illustration below.

The first value of 33 was put into place using the Linear Dimension option (see facing page toolbar illustration) and the 45 value was input using the Continue option. AutoCAD LT 2000 automatically lines up the 45 value with the 33 value. This is what 'Continue' does. To try this, draw a shape similar to that shown below. Here are the steps:

1 Place the 33 on the first line segment in the usual way using the Linear option (your value does not have to be 33).

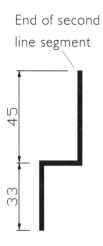

End of second line segment

2 Now select the Continue option. AutoCAD LT asks: 'Specify second extension line origin' (not a first!). Pick the end of the second line segment. The dimension line aligns correctly. Press Enter twice to end the command.

Using Continue on existing dimensions

If you try to use Continue on a dimension you did some time ago (say during a previous drawing session), AutoCAD LT 2000 asks you to pick the dimension you want to 'continue' from by prompting 'Select continued dimension'. Pick the existing dimension and proceed as above when you see the prompt: 'Second extension line origin'.

Position the first dimension with care as AutoCAD LT 2000 aligns all the other dimensions to it.

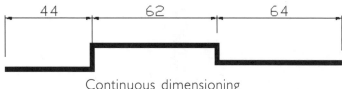

44   62   64

Continuous dimensioning

Baseline Dimensioning

Baseline dimensioning refers all dimensions back to a datum line. The dimensions are stacked one above the other. The distance separating the dimensions is controlled by the system variable DIMDLI.

A datum line is a common reference point.

You may also control it using the Geometry option of the Dimensioning styles (see page 146). To try Baseline dimensioning, draw a line like the one below. Here are the steps involved:

1 Place the 175.5 dimension value on the first segment using the Linear Dimension option (your value does not have to be 175.5).

Datum line

2 Click on the Baseline icon and respond to the prompt: 'Specify a second extension line origin' by using Object Snap to pick at point B in the illustration.

3 The dimension line is positioned a preset distance (which can be changed) away from the first dimension line.

B

4 AutoCAD LT again asks: 'Specify second extension line origin'. Pick point C and press Enter twice to finish the command.

C

Angular

Angular Dimensioning

Acute and obtuse angles can be measured using the Angular Dimensioning option. Draw some lines in the shape of 'z' to practice applying angular dimensions.

1 Click on the Angular icon (see toolbar illustration on facing page).

2 In response to 'select arc, circle or line', click on a line.

3 To the second response 'Second line', select the second line.
As you move the cursor AutoCAD LT offers you various dimensioning formats. Try moving the cursor along the area within the acute angle and click when you like a format you see.

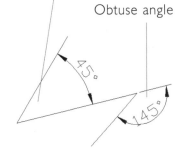

Acute angle

Obtuse angle

Try the same for the obtuse angle. All the angles below are placed by moving the cursor into different positions.

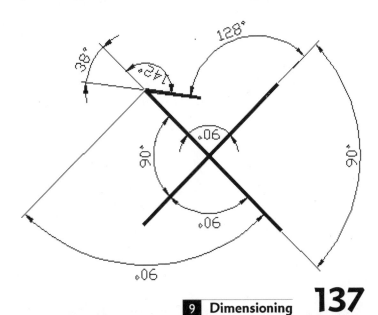

When the Angular Dimension option is selected, the prompt asks: 'Select arc, circle, line, or press ENTER:'. The effect of choosing the circle is illustrated below: just pick two points on the circle to measure the angle between them. Similarly, the sweep of an arc can be measured thus:

The term arrow in dimension-ing is used to describe any symbol at the end of a dimension or leader line. That includes ticks and dots.

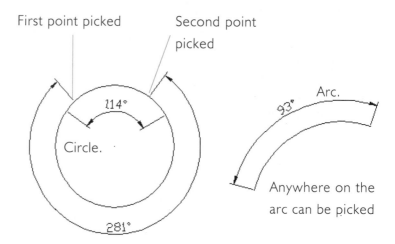

First point picked

Second point picked

Arc.

114°

Circle.

93°

281°

Anywhere on the arc can be picked

Leader Lines

Leader lines are used to add annotations to drawings. The Toolbar offers the Quick Leader option considered here. Leader lines can be created with or without arrows; they may also have straight lines or splines. A leader has a flat section for text called a 'landing' or 'dogleg'.

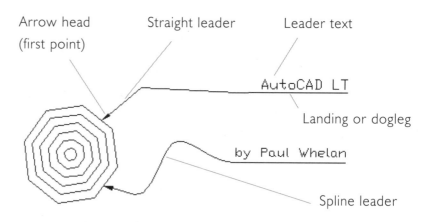

Arrow head (first point)

Straight leader

Leader text

AutoCAD LT

Landing or dogleg

by Paul Whelan

Spline leader

...cont'd

To place a leader line in a drawing, follow the steps below:

The leader arrows and text size can be set in a dimension style.

1 Select the Leader icon. AutoCAD LT asks: 'Specify first leader point:'. Pick a point in the usual way (Object Snap is available).

2 By default you are given an arrowhead and asked to pick the second point. Do so and press Enter. This defines the leader line.

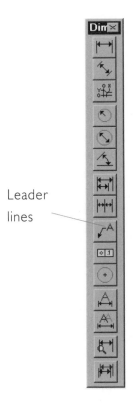

Leader lines

3 AutoCAD now asks you to specify the text width. Leave it at 0 (just press Enter). The default option now is to enter the <Mtext>. The mtext (multiline text) prompt displays. Type in the text you want and pick OK to finish the command.

Some of the other options

If you type Leader at the command prompt the resulting options are different than from Quick Leader on the Toolbar. Here are some of the options:

- **Format:** This option is chosen by typing 'f' for format. Under it, you find the options to use a 'Spline' or change back to a 'Straight Leader Line'. The arrow can be removed by selecting 'None'. You may exit the format options list by typing 'e' for exit.

- **Annotation:** Press Enter twice when this default is offered to see the options for: 'Tolerances', 'Copy', 'Block', 'None' and 'mtext'.

Editing a Dimension

Text that is part of a dimension cannot be edited with the normal text commands 'mtext' and 'dtext'. AutoCAD LT provides several ways to edit dimension text:

Command line: 'dimtedit'

Menu: Dimensions > Align Text

Use Grips

Dimensions > Align Text

When you click on an option such as 'Left', AutoCAD LT asks you to select the dimension. When you do so, the text is left aligned.

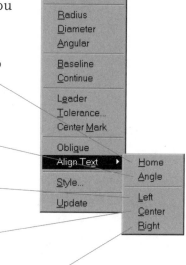

Returns any re-positioned text to the way it was before moving

Positions text at the angle entered

Pushes text to the left end of a dimension line

Places text in the centre of a dimension line

Places text to the right end of a dimension line

All the dimensions here were originally centred, but after editing some are left-aligned and rotated 45 degrees

 If you are constantly editing dimensions, consider setting up a dimensioning style.

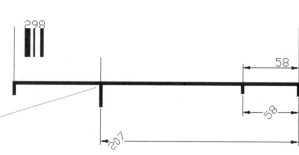

...cont'd

You can select several dimensions at once and apply the edit changes to all the dimensions.

Typing 'dimtedit' at the command line offers the same options of Left, Right, Center, Home and Angle. However, it also allows you to reposition the text using the cursor. Try executing the command now. AutoCAD LT asks you to select the text for editing.

The moment the dimension is selected the dimension text moves with the cursor. Simply pick a new location to reposition it. The extension lines also follow the cursor movement so that you can lengthen or shorten them.

This dimension had the text moved to a new position and the extension lines stretched. See the original dimension on the previous page.

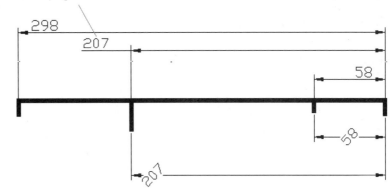

Using Grips to edit a dimension

Click on the dimension when the command line is blank. The Grips then appear. Notice the Grip at the centre point of the text. This Grip can be selected by clicking on it. A selected Grip becomes red in colour. The text can then be moved into position.

This Grip can be used to move the text or stretch the extension lines

The DIMEDIT Command

Dimedit allows you to easily replace dimension text. Type the command at the command line. Each of the options is described here.

Home: Returns the text to the position it occupied before it was moved.

Rotate: Rotates the dimension text.

Oblique: Repositions the extension lines at a new angle. The default position is at 90 degrees to the dimension line. An obliquing angle of 45 degrees is shown in the illustration below.

Extension lines may be controlled by setting up a dimension style.

New: Allows you to replace the dimension text. Once the option New is selected, the Multiline Text Editor opens. Just type the new text in the editor and click OK. The old text is represented by <>. To remove the old text you must remove these symbols in the Multiline Text Editor.

These extension lines are set to an angle of 45 degrees using the oblique option

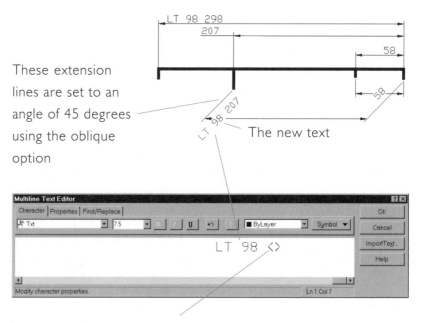

The new text

The markers '< >' symbolise the old text. If you leave these here the old text remains

Dimension Styles and Tolerances

The various settings which control how a dimension appears can be stored as a dimension style. Several different styles may be created and used when needed. This chapter shows you how to create these styles.

Covers

Chapter Ten

Dimension Styles

All elements that make up a dimension can be modified to form a dimension style.

For example, you might have oblique extension lines with dimension text always above the line.

These settings can be saved with a name and later applied when dimensioning objects.

Styles give a drawing or a project visual consistency.

Menu: Dimensions > Style...

The Dimension Style Manager dialog box is used to define a style.

Dimension
Linear
Aligned
Ordinate
Radius
Diameter
Angular
Baseline
Continue
Leader
Tolerance...
Center Mark
Oblique
Align Text ▶
Style...
Update

The style in use

Displays a preview of the style as it is created

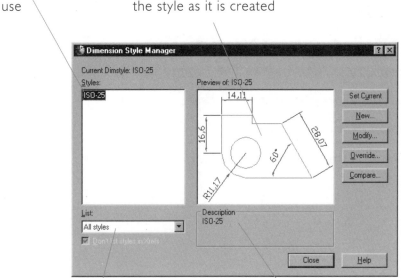

This filter allows you to control the display of existing styles

Displays a description of the current style

How to Create a Style

The following steps illustrate how a basic style is created. This style is used to dimension the exterior of a building as shown on an architectural drawing.

Its basic features are to use a tick instead of an arrow and to place the dimension text on the left extension line, as shown in the illustration.

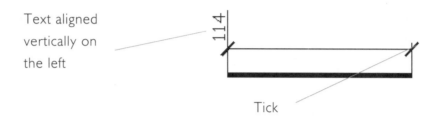

Text aligned vertically on the left

Tick

| From the drop-down menu click on Dimension > Style...

2 The Dimension Style Manager dialog box appears. Pick on the New button.

A new style can be created from an existing style. This allows you to build up a library of styles without having to define all the elements each time.

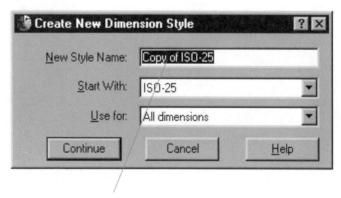

3 The Create New Dimension Style box displays. Type in 'Exterior' and pick on the Continue button.

The New Dimesion Style dialog box displays. This allows you to define the elements that make up the style. Some of these elements are examined on the following pages.

Arrows & Lines Settings

The geometry settings control the appearance of dimension lines, extension lines, arrow heads and centre marks.

The 1st extension line is the first point you selected when dimensioning the object.

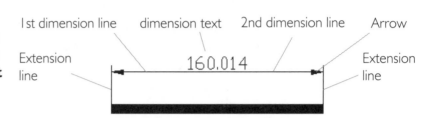

1st dimension line   dimension text   2nd dimension line   Arrow

Extension line   Extension line

160.014

Setting a colour allows you to specify a pen thickness at plot time

Refers to the baseline offsets

Click to select different 'arrows'

Lineweight can be displayed on screen in LT 2000

'Suppressing the 1st' tells AutoCAD LT not to draw the first half of the dimension line

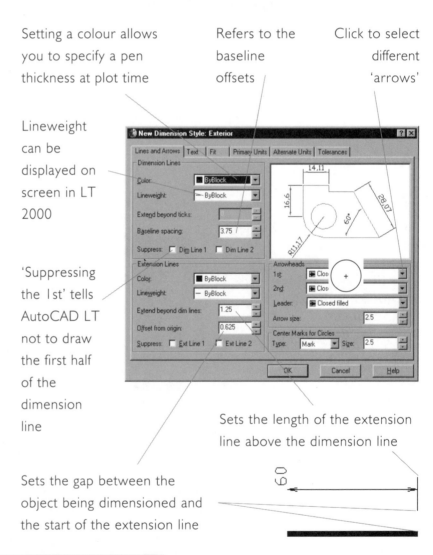

Sets the length of the extension line above the dimension line

Sets the gap between the object being dimensioned and the start of the extension line

Arrows & Lines Examples

Here are some styles based on modifications to the Line & Arrows tab options in the New Dimension Style dialog box.

Any of these features can be saved as a new dimension style.

First extension line suppressed

Extension line 'Origin Offset' increased

Extension line increased

Both extension lines suppressed

Dots instead of arrows

Extension line decreased

Dimension line suppressed

Circle

Spacing (under the Dimension Line in the Geometry dialog box)

Centre mark

Centre line

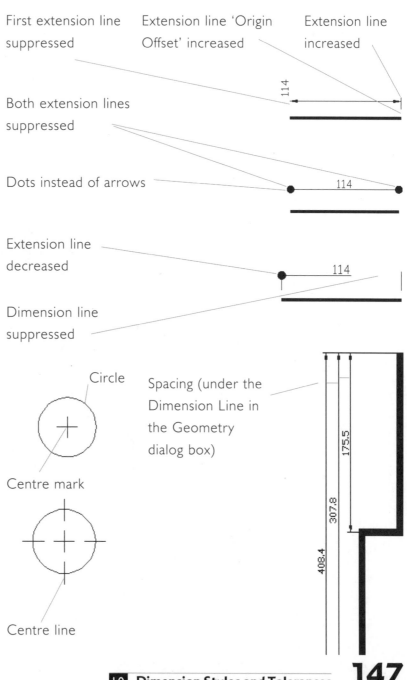

Some Text Tab Settings

The Text Tab on the New Dimension Style dialog box allows you to control text style and where the text appears on the dimension.

Select an existing text style from the down arrow or pick on the three dots button to define a new style

Height of the dimension text – given in the drawing units

Controls the alignment of the dimension text – pick on the buttons to see the effect

Sets the colour of the text. This is useful if you have a pen thickness assigned to a colour

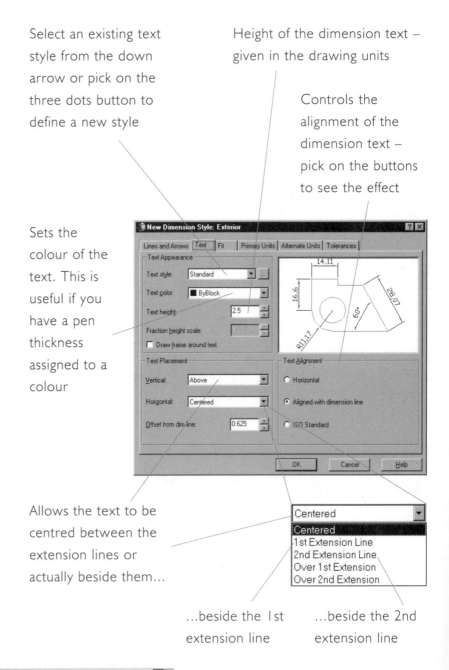

Allows the text to be centred between the extension lines or actually beside them...

...beside the 1st extension line

...beside the 2nd extension line

Fit Tab Examples

These examples show the affect of the Fit options under the Fit Tab. AutoCAD LT attempts to carry out what you have set if it is possible, otherwise AutoCAD LT decides what looks best.

No leader line is requested here

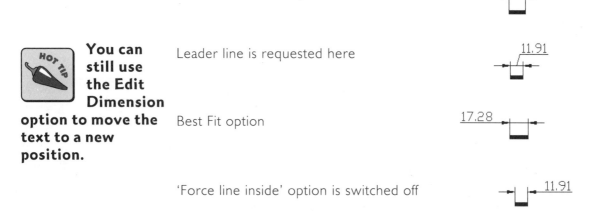

You can still use the Edit Dimension option to move the text to a new position.

Leader line is requested here

Best Fit option

'Force line inside' option is switched off

This dialog box is dynamic. As you select the various buttons, the preview updates.

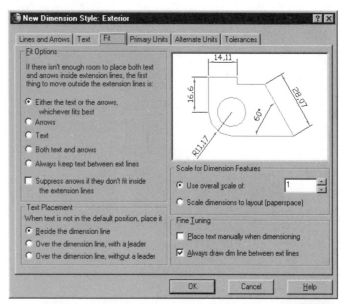

Some Primary Units Settings

Primary units are the units with which you create your drawing. You either set them up in the DDUNITS dialog box or use the Setup Wizard. You can control how these are displayed in dimensions here in the Primary Units tab.

Sets the number of decimal places displayed in a dimension

You can change the set primary units here by picking the down arrow and choosing another option

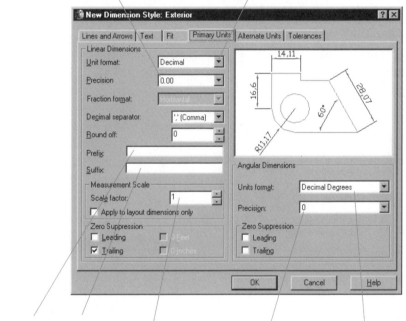

Allows a prefix or suffix such as 'mm' to accompany the dimension text

Allows you to scale the overall size of the dimension style – it is the old DIMSTYLE

Selects the degree of precision – pick on the down arrow

The method for measuring angles may be defined here

Primary & Alternative Tab Examples

Increased text height

Precision is 0.0

Increased gap

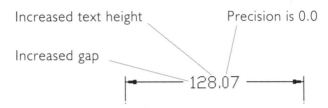

128.07

When a style is updated, any existing dimensions in that style are also updated.

Alternate units enabled – feet & inches

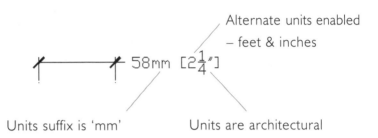

58mm [2¼"]

Units suffix is 'mm'

Units are architectural

Suffix is set to 'all lengths'

Precision 0.00

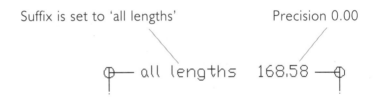

all lengths   168.58

Units suffix is 'mm'

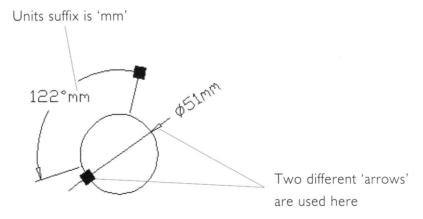

122°mm

ø51mm

Two different 'arrows' are used here

Styles Using Tolerances

The number of decimal places shown in the dimension text and the tolerance can be set independently.

Tolerances can be added to a dimension style. A tolerance can show the range of error or acceptability in the manufacture of a product. Tolerance settings are found in Tolerance Tab. The Tolerance options used by AutoCAD LT 2000 are displayed below:

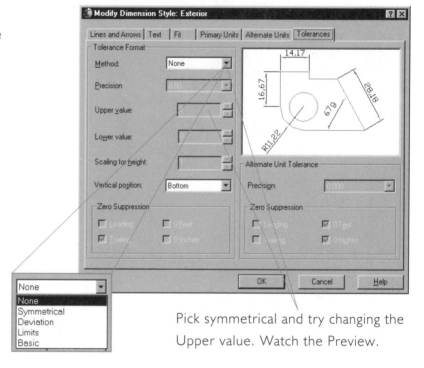

Pick symmetrical and try changing the Upper value. Watch the Preview.

A suffix or prefix attached to a dimension also shows on a tolerance. This may make the dimensioning text a little too long!

Symmetrical:	values are given the same upper and lower limit
Deviation:	a variation that has a different plus and minus value
Limits:	actually adds/subtracts values you specify to the dimension text value
Basic:	places a box around the basic dimension text value

The number of decimal points shown in the tolerances is controlled by the Primary Units button 'Units'.

Examples of Tolerances

Symmetrical: values are given the same upper and lower limit of 0.5.

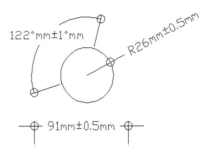

Deviation: a variation that has a different plus and minus value. The plus value is 1 and the minus value is 0.

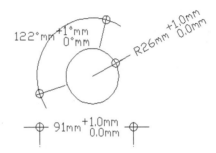

Basic: places a box around the basic dimension text value.

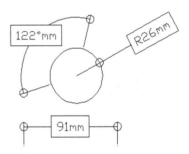

Limits: actually adds/ subtracts values you specify to the dimension text value, in this case 0.8 is added and 0.4 is subtracted from the correctly measured dimension value.

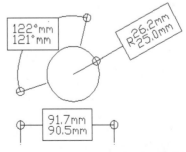

Using Dimension Styles

In this example, three dimensioning styles have been created: one for the exterior of a building, another for the interior and the third for adding annotations.

List of
dimension
styles

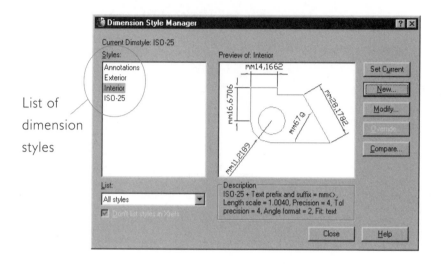

Any style can be used as the basis for a following style, so ensure the style you have in the 'Current' box is what you want, before you make modifications to define a new style.

If you set up a template file, define all your styles within it so that your styles are available for all your drawings.

Modifications to a Style

Styles may be modified at any time. Simply highlight the style you want to change and then pick the Modify button. All settings for that style are then made available.

Copying Styles

Dimension styles can be copied from one drawing to another using the Design Center. To discover more information about working with the Design Center, see Chapter 8.

Attribute Creation

In this chapter, you'll learn how to attribute text to graphical images. This text can hold information about a drawing and may later be separated from the drawing objects and placed into a word processor, spreadsheet or database application as a bill of materials.

Covers

Chapter Eleven

What is an Attribute?

The creation and insertion of Blocks into a drawing speeds up the drawing process considerably and adds consistency to drawings. Frequently, it's necessary to insert text beside a Block to indicate its characteristics.

For example, when drawing an electric circuit, the symbol for a battery may be inserted as a Block and later the voltage may need to be added in as text beside it.

An attribute is text attached to a Block.

Instead of writing the voltage in as text beside the Block (using dtext for example) each time the text is inserted, AutoCAD LT allows you to attribute the text to the Block. This implies that each time the Block is inserted the text is also inserted.

The use of attributes can be even more sophisticated. For example, an attribute may be defined so that AutoCAD LT asks you for the voltage each time the Block is inserted.

At a later stage the voltage value can be extracted from the drawing and used in another program such as a word processor, database or spreadsheet. It is this ability to extract information from a Block that makes the concept of attributes so valuable.

More than one attribute can be attached to a Block.

Attributes can be defined as textual data attached to a Block. In the example below, a Block of a wheel has four different attributes attached to it. When the wheel is inserted into the drawing, AutoCAD LT asks: 'How many spokes?', 'Lightweight or Heavyweight?', 'Diameter of the wheel?' and 'The Cost?'.

These kinds of question are programmed in by you, the user. You can learn how to do this in the following pages.

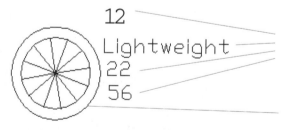

Each one is a user-defined attribute attached to the wheel

Block of a wheel

Creating your First Attribute

AutoCAD LT asks you for some specific information when you define an attribute. The most important criteria are explained below.

A tag: a common example of a tag can be seen by looking at any official form you might fill in for, say, tax purposes. The box in which you type in your name will be preceded by the word 'Name:'. 'Name:', in this context, is a tag in AutoCAD LT language.

You should be familiar with Blocks before you work with attributes.

A prompt: is the question or comment you want to appear when the Block is being inserted. For example: 'What is your name?'

A value: is the default value and would be the most common value you may use. For example, for the bicycle wheels, the company might manufacture more 28" wheels than any other size, so here, 28" would be a sensible default value.

The mode: concerns the visibility of the attribute value on the screen. You can define an attribute as being invisible. If you do so then you must switch the attribute visibility on if you wish to see it at a later stage. An attribute can also be defined as constant. In this case AutoCAD LT does not ask for a value when you insert the Block.

If you want to use a text style other than STANDARD, you should define it before trying to create attributes.

The remaining steps used in defining an attribute are similar to Block creation and text insertion.

The insertion point refers to the point at which the Block is attached to the cross-hairs when the Block is being placed into the drawing. Use Object Snap to accurately select a Block.

Text options are the usual ones of justification, text height and rotation. To use a text style, remember you must define it first.

The following pages describe attribute creation in detail.

Steps to Attribute Creation

1 To complete the exercise outlined in the following few pages, before you start defining the attributes, draw a simplified wheel similar to that on page 156.

2 From the Draw drop-down menu click on Block and then Define Attributes...

Block ▸	Make...
Point ▸	Base
Hatch...	Define Attributes...
Boundary...	
Region	

Attributes can also be created by typing ATTDEF at the command line.

3 The Attribute Definition dialog box appears with the cursor flashing in the Tag edit box. Type in the tag: 'spoke_no'. Do not use spaces.

4 Next type in the prompt you want to appear on the screen when you insert the Block of the wheel, for example: 'How many spokes?'

Type the tag here   Text here appears when the Block is being inserted   Default number of spokes

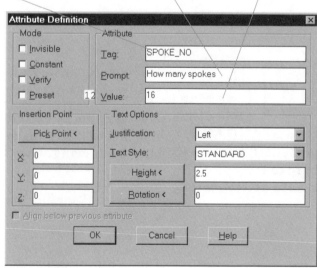

...cont'd

You can proceed to the next page after Step 8 if you want to see the single attribute in action.

5 If more '12-spoke' type wheels are made than any other: 12 would then be a wise default value. AutoCAD LT then offers this value when you insert the Block. You can of course override it. Type in 12 in the Value edit box.

6 Now select the position for the tag beside the wheel. In the Insertion point section of the dialog box, click on the 'Pick Point <' button. You are then returned to the drawing. Pick a point to the right and just above the wheel (around the 2 o'clock position). You are then returned to the dialog box.

An attribute can be defined as invisible by picking Invisible in the Mode section of the dialog box.

7 In the Text Options section, select 'Height' and tell AutoCAD LT the height of the text by picking a point just above the insertion point.

8 Leave the rotation angle at 0 (horizontal) and click on OK. You have finished defining the first attribute for the number of spokes. Your screen should now look like this:

The defined attribute: the tag is left visible until you 'Block it' later

SPOKE_NO

Now define the other attributes. Give them the following specifications and then click on 'Invisible' in the Mode category, after each specification:

Tag – WEIGHT;   Value – Lightweight

Tag – DIAMETER;   Value – 22

Tag – PRICE;   Value – 56

Lastly, to Block the wheel and attributes, see overleaf.

Creating a Block with Attributes

When you have defined the four attributes, your AutoCAD LT screen looks like this:

```
SPOKE_NO
WEIGHT
DIAMETER
PRICE
```

You now need to Block the wheel and the attributes:

You can redefine Blocks and attach attributes to them.

| From the Draw drop-down menu, click on Block followed by, Make...

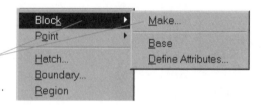

2 Enter the name: 'wheel' and click on Select objects and press Enter. Then pick your Base point.

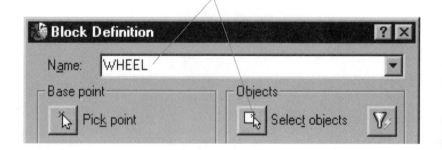

AutoCAD LT warns you that a Block already exists if you try to redefine it.

3 AutoCAD LT pulls a selection box around both the wheel and the attributes. Click on Apply and then Close.

Inserting a Block with Attributes

To ensure that your computer and this text block are using the same settings, set the system variable ATTDIA to 1 (use the command line).

A Block can be inserted by typing 'insert' at the command line.

1 From the Insert menu, click on Block...

2 Select the Block, 'wheel' and click OK. AutoCAD LT asks for the scaling on the X and Y axes and the rotation angle. Press Enter to accept the defaults.

3 The Enter Attributes dialog box displays showing the default values you entered when you defined the attributes. You can accept these by clicking on OK or edit each of the values as desired.

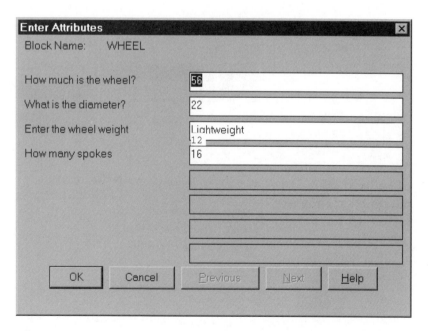

4 The Block displays with the attributes beside it. Notice that the value Lightweight did not appear because it was defined as being invisible. However, it can be made visible.

Visibility of Attributes

Attributes may eventually clutter a drawing. However, their visibility can be controlled. Three options are available:

If you have been given a drawing created by someone else, try checking the visibility of attributes. They may have simply been switched off.

1 'Normal' mode refers to the way an attribute is defined. If 'Invisible' is ticked in the Mode option in the Attribute Definition dialog box, then in normal mode this is invisible.

2 'On' makes all attributes visible, regardless of how they were originally defined.

3 'Off' makes all the attributes invisible, regardless of how they were originally defined.

The visibility of the attributes is controlled from the View drop-down menu. Click on View > Display > Attribute Display.

You cannot control the visibility of individual attributes: they are either all on, off or normal.

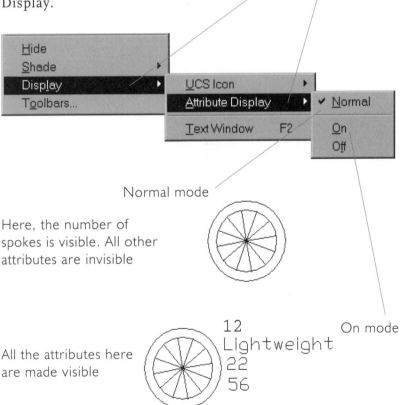

Normal mode

Here, the number of spokes is visible. All other attributes are invisible

On mode

12
Lightweight
22
56

All the attributes here are made visible

Attribute Editing and Extraction

In this chapter, the procedure for editing attribute values in a drawing is explained. Also, the important step of extracting data from a drawing is treated in detail. This is the procedure for creating a Bill of Materials.

Covers

Chapter Twelve

Attribute Editing

After a Block with attributes has been inserted, you may need to change the values in the attribute. You can do this to the attributes individually or globally. To edit attribute values individually, follow the steps below:

1 From the Modify menu select Object > Attribute > Single...

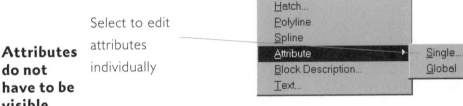

Select to edit
attributes
individually

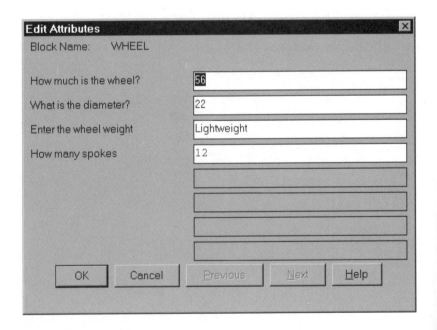

Attributes do not have to be visible beside the Block in order to edit them.

2 The command line prompts you to select the Block containing the attributes. Select a Block. The Edit Attributes dialog box appears.

3 Click on the attribute value you want to change to highlight it, then change it. Click OK when you finish.

...cont'd

Attributes can be edited globally. This means that all values in a particular tag can be changed from the existing values to new ones.

Suppose you want to change all the values 'Lightweight' to 'Featherweight'. Carry out the following steps:

1 From the Modify menu select Object > Attribute > Global.

If you forget the name of a tag, just explode the Block and the tag names are displayed. Write them down and then undo the Explode command to proceed.

2 Read the command line carefully during this operation. The prompt is 'Edit attributes one at a time? <Y>'. Type N for no and press Enter.

3 The prompt now reads 'Edit only attributes visible on the screen? <Y>'. Type N for no and press Enter.

4 AutoCAD LT 2000 now wants to know the 'Block name specification'. In other words, type in the name of the Block – 'wheel' in this example – and press Enter.

5 Now type in the tag name you are interested in modifying globally. In this example it is 'weight'. Press Enter.

6 Next, enter the value you want to change – in this example it is 'Lightweight' – and press Enter.

7 AutoCAD LT 2000 tells you how many attributes it finds and then asks you for the 'String to change'. A string is a group of letters. Type in 'Light' and press Enter.

8 You now see the prompt 'New String'. Type in 'Heavy'. AutoCAD LT 2000 then converts 'Lightweight' to 'Heavyweight'.

Attribute Extraction – Overview

When a drawing is finished, it may be desirable to separate all the values attached to Blocks and use them in a word processor, or some other application such as a database or spreadsheet. This, in effect, is the method for creating a bill of materials.

For example, if a drawing contains seventy or eighty wheels with the attributes defined in the previous chapter, you may like to discover the total cost of all the wheels.

To do this, you must separate the values from the drawing of the wheel. This is called attribute extraction.

 AutoCAD LT can also tell you the number of Blocks in the drawing when you are extracting values from any tag.

In the following few pages, we'll examine how to do this. An overview of the steps involved is given below.

1 You must write a special file to tell AutoCAD LT which tags you want the values to be extracted from. This is called an extract file. Write the extract file in Windows Notepad and give it the filename extension '.txt'.

2 Next, tell AutoCAD LT which Blocks you want these values extracted from.

3 Data can be taken out in different ways. You need to tell AutoCAD LT the format you want the data to be in.

4 Now supply AutoCAD LT with the name of the file into which you want it to put the extracted values. This file is called the extract file.

5 Lastly, look at the extract file AutoCAD LT creates for you. If it is error free, you can then place the data into another application.

Attribute Extraction – in Detail

Let's assume that you have ten wheels in the drawing and that you want to extract the values in the PRICE tag, then place them in a spreadsheet to total the prices.

If you have forgotten what the tags are, just explode a Block. Use Undo to return back to a Block.

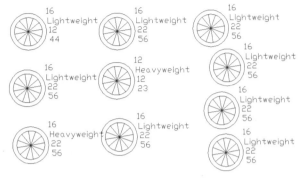

For this procedure, never put in a space at the end of a line in Windows Notepad.

1 Start your Windows Notepad text editor. This is usually available under Accessories in Windows. Be very careful typing into the editor, especially when you reach the end of a line – never put in a space at the end of a line!

2 Type what is shown in the illustration below. Use upper-case letters for consistency.

3 Save the file with the name 'price.txt' into a folder where you can find it later. If you are unsure where to put it, try the root of C (C:\). Note, you must give the file the extension '.txt'.

This gives you the Block name

This gives the number of Blocks

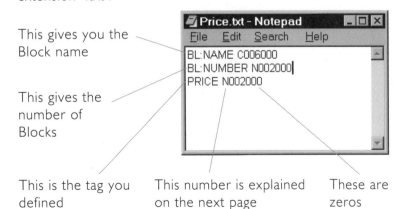

A detailed explanation of the codes in this template file is provided on page 172.

This is the tag you defined

This number is explained on the next page

These are zeros

4 The template file you wrote in Notepad is used in Step 6. To start the extraction process, click on the Tools drop-down menu and then Attribute Extraction. The Attribute Extraction dialog box displays.

Leave this here. It is the extract file AutoCAD LT makes for you. It holds the values. Its name is the same as the drawing name, with the filename extension '.txt'

5 CDF means that each value has commas around it. Use this option.

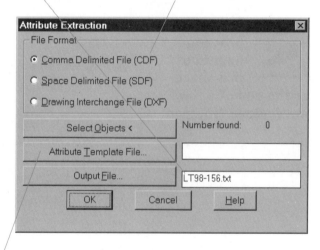

6 Click on Attribute Template File and find the file PRICE.TXT that you created in Windows Notepad.

7 Click on Select Objects <. AutoCAD LT prompts: Select objects at the command line. Type ALL and press Enter (or drag a box around all the Blocks).

8 If you are successful, AutoCAD LT 2000 tells you that you have 10 records in the extract file at the command line. If you have an error, look at the template file you wrote in Notepad. It may be flawed.

Viewing the Extract File

To check if the extract file contains the values you want, you must open it. It has the extension '.txt', which means that you can open it in Windows Notepad. Here is the one you should find after carrying out the eight steps:

The first column
contains the name
of the Block

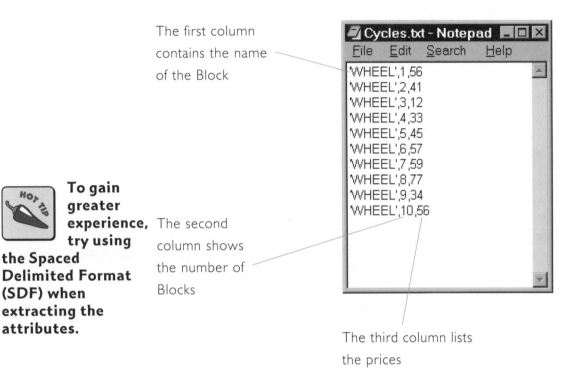

To gain greater experience, The second try using the Spaced Delimited Format (SDF) when extracting the attributes.

The second
column shows
the number of
Blocks

The third column lists
the prices

Each column of data is separated by a comma. This is the result of the Comma Delimited Format (CDF) you selected at the time of extraction.

Importing the Extract File into Excel

The extract file can be inserted into another program. As an example, we will place it into the spreadsheet program Microsoft Excel (which is a part of the Microsoft Office suite) as follows:

1 Start the Excel program. With a blank sheet on the screen, click on File > Open.

2 In the Open dialog box select Text Files from the options under 'Files of type:'.

If you are familiar with Copy & Paste, try using it to place the extract file into Excel, or some other program.

3 Now look for the extract file: 'cycles.txt' in this example.

4 Excel opens the Text Import Wizard to help you make the right choices to successfully import the file.

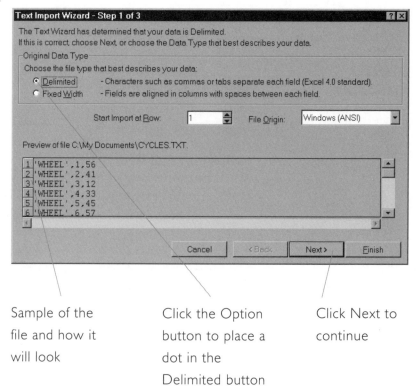

Sample of the file and how it will look

Click the Option button to place a dot in the Delimited button

Click Next to continue

5 Click on Next to proceed. Wizard Step 2 of 3 appears. Place a tick in the 'Comma' box and remove the tick from any other box.

6 Click on Next. Wizard Step 3 of 3 appears. Place a dot in the 'General' Option button and select Finish.

At this stage, the data in the extract file should fall into three columns in the Excel spreadsheet as shown below. The spreadsheet has been simply formatted with column titles and the total calculated.

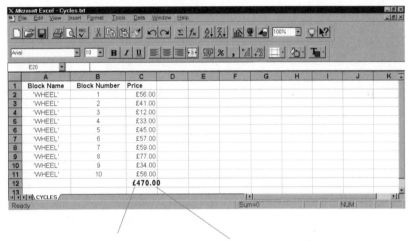

The drawing contains wheels valued at £470

Here is the formula that was used in this example:
=sum(C2:C11)

Template File Codes

Template file contents

Line 1	BL:NAME C006000
Line 2	BL:NUMBER N002000
Line 3	PRICE N002000

Line 1

BL:NAME tells AutoCAD LT to put the Block name in the extract file. The C006000 code is made up of three parts:

1   The first part is the letter 'C'. Shows the data to be extracted is in the form of alphanumeric characters.

2   The second part of the code consists of the following three digits, '006'. These tell AutoCAD LT that the name of the Block is not longer than 6 characters.

3   The third part of the code is '000'. This tells AutoCAD LT that there are no decimal places involved.

Line 2

BL:NUMBER tells AutoCAD LT to put the number of Blocks in the drawing into the extract file. The N002000 code is made up of three parts:

1   The first part is the letter 'N'. This means that the data to be extracted is in the form of numbers only. These numbers can be used in mathematical operations later on if you wish.

2   The second part of the code consists of the next three digits, '002'. These tell AutoCAD LT that the number of the Block is not longer than 2 characters.

3   The third part of the code is '000'. This tells AutoCAD LT that there are no decimal places used.

Line 3

PRICE is the tag you defined. You could include other tags in the file if you wanted to extract their values. Because PRICE is a number upon which you might later make a calculation (e.g. you might total these values) you start the code with 'N'.

Hatching, Plotting and Viewports

AutoCAD LT 2000 provides a command to apply hatch patterns to a drawing. Hatching is associative: it is associated with the objects that form its boundary. You will also learn to define your own text styles, set up different views of a drawing and finally to print a finished drawing.

Covers

Chapter Thirteen

Hatching

How the command works

The Hatch command allows you to fill an area with either a solid fill or a hatch pattern. AutoCAD LT 2000 has a library of predefined hatch patterns that symbolise materials such as steel, clay, brass or concrete.

You may also define simple patterns yourself (user-defined) or create a custom design from scratch using simple trigonometry.

This latter custom design is beyond the scope of this text. Lastly, a solid area of colour can be applied to an enclosed area. This colour is defined by the colour of the layer the hatching is on.

Always place hatching on its own separate layer.

Command line: bhatch

Menu: Draw > Hatch

Toolbar:

The command in action

On issuing the command, you need to select or define a hatch pattern. Then select the area you want to fill with the pattern.

A drawing with a lot of hatching can take a considerable amount of time to regenerate.

Lastly, you may test the pattern to see if it is correct and then apply it if you are satisfied with its appearance. Some hatch patterns are shown here:

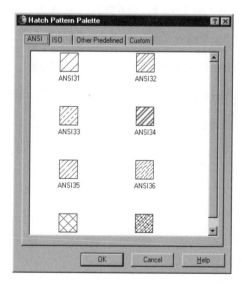

Applying a Hatch Pattern

To follow these steps, set up a drawing page of 420mm by 297mm and draw a shape similar to that shown below.

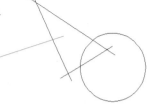

You'll apply a hatch here

1 Issue the command from the drop-down menu or type BHATCH at the command line. The Boundary Hatch dialog box appears.

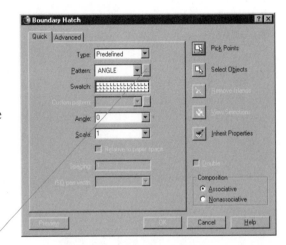

2 Click here to see the available patterns.

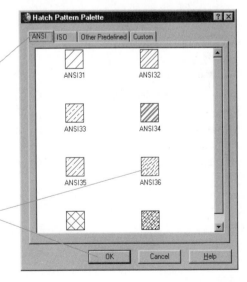

3 Pick the ANSI tab.

4 Select Pattern ANSI 136 and pick OK.

...cont'd

If you select too big a scale, the pattern may not show when it is applied.

5 Type 1.0 here.

6 To define the area to hatch, select Pick Points.

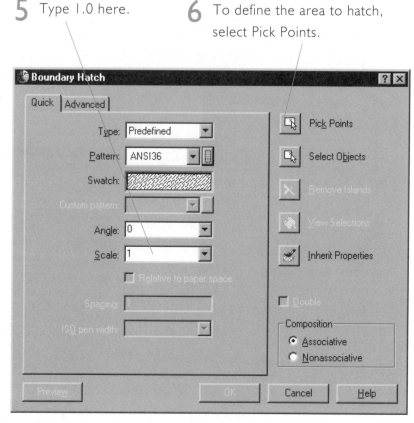

At Step 9 you could return to the dialog box and change the scale setting to view the effect.

7 Pick here. The boundary around the point you pick is highlighted. Press Enter.

Cursor

8 The Boundary Hatch dialog box returns. Click on the Preview button.

9 If you are satisfied with the preview at this stage, press Enter to return to the Hatch dialog box, then click on OK.

Hatch Patterns and Design Center

The Design Center can be used to drag hatch patterns into a drawing (see page 119 for an explanation of the Design Center). To drag a hatch pattern into the drawing, follow the steps below.

1 Click on the Load icon folder and look for the Support folder.

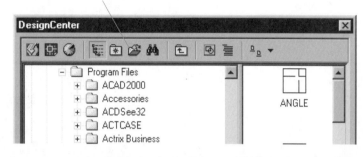

Before dragging a hatch pattern onto a drawing, double-click on it to check its properties.

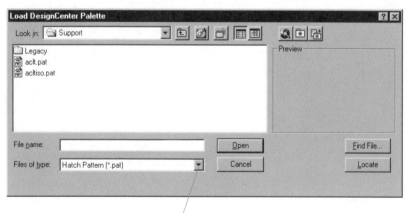

2 Pick on the PAT type of file.

3 ACLT and ACLTISO hatch pattern libraries are then displayed.

4 Pick ACLTISO and pick Open. The hatch patterns in that library display 'visually' in the Design Center. Drag the one you want onto the drawing.

Text Styles

AutoCAD LT 2000 comes with a STANDARD text style. You can define your own styles and use them while inserting text into the drawing or a part of the dimensioning style.

Here are the steps for creating a style called EXTERIOR:

1 From the Format drop-down menu select Text Style... The Text Style dialog box appears. Define the style you want in this box.

2 Click on New.

Standard AutoCAD LT style

The font on which the style is based

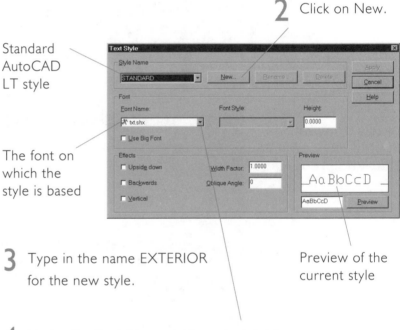

Preview of the current style

3 Type in the name EXTERIOR for the new style.

4 Under the Font Name option select Arial.

5 Leave the Height setting at 0. This means that AutoCAD LT asks you for the height of the text every time you use a text command.

6 Click on Apply. The new style is created.

Using a New Style

The new style EXTERIOR created on the previous page is now offered as an option in any command that uses text styles.

Try the following:

1 From the Dimension drop-down menu, select Style...

2 In the Dimension Style Manager dialog box click on Modify. Select the Text tab.

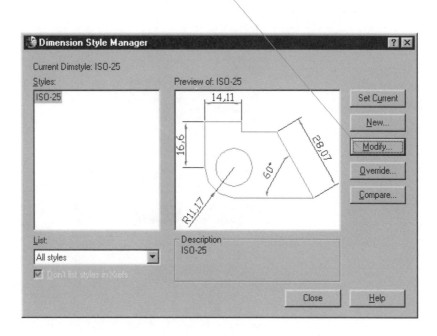

3 Under the Text tab, pick the down-arrow after 'Text Style...'. You will see the style EXTERIOR that you created on the previous page.

Similarly, if you run the mtext command, the EXTERIOR style appears under the properties tab, allowing you to use it as a text style.

Viewports

When you create a drawing in AutoCAD LT, you are working in Model Space. Model Space initially gives you a single view of a drawing.

You can view the drawing in several different ways if you divide the Model Space screen into several viewports. To do this:

1 Open a drawing in the usual way. Try opening the 'Electric Train' drawing in the Samples folder. It opens into a single view in Model Space.

2 From the View drop-down menu, select Viewports.

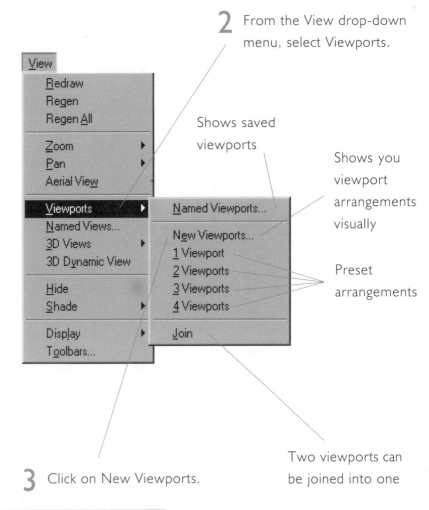

Shows saved viewports

Shows you viewport arrangements visually

Preset arrangements

Two viewports can be joined into one

3 Click on New Viewports.

...cont'd

Right & Left
refer to which
viewport will be
the largest

Above & Below
refer to which
viewport will
be the largest

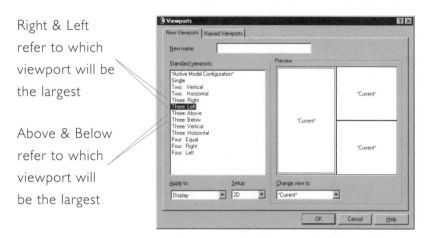

4 Select 'Three: Left'. Your screen divides into three tiled viewports, each one showing the same view of the drawing.

5 Move the cross-hairs from one viewport to another and the cross-hairs change to an arrow. The active or current viewport is the one with the cross-hairs. To make another viewport active, just click in the one you want.

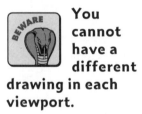

You cannot have a different drawing in each viewport.

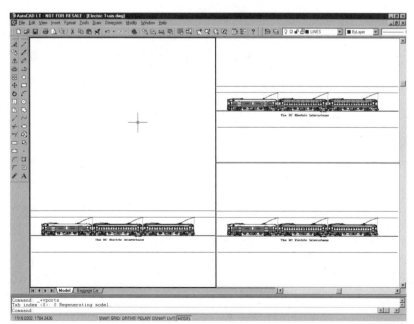

...cont'd

6 When a viewport is active, you can draw and edit in it in the normal way.

7 Each viewport can have a different setting for the zoom level, grid and snap. The image below shows three different levels of zoom.

You can start a command in one tiled viewport and finish it in another.

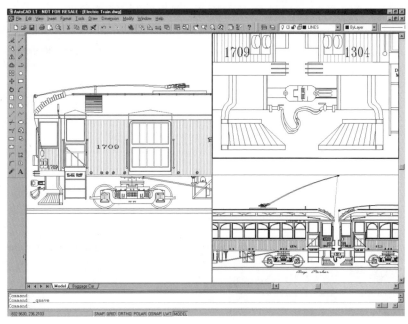

8 A command can be started in one viewport and continued in another. Try drawing a line from one to another. Remember that you start the command in an active viewport and when you move to the inactive port you must click first to make it active.

9 To return to a single viewport, select the View drop-down menu, then Tiled Viewports and finally I Viewport. The view that appears in the single port is the current or active one.

Saving and Restoring Tiled Viewports

Once the viewports are arranged suitably you can save the configuration. This allows you to return to the same arrangement any time the drawing is opened. The Restore option allows you to restore a pre-saved arrangement.

To save an arrangement follow these steps.

Saving and restoring viewports can speed up work on large complex drawings.

1 Set up an arrangement of tiled viewports as shown on pages 181/ 182.

2 From the View drop-down menu select Viewports.

3 Click New Viewports.

4 In the New Name box, type a name such as LINKAGE.

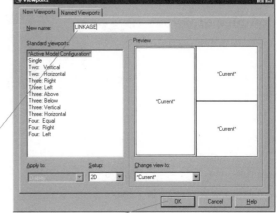

5 Click on OK to save the arrangement with this name.

Now return to a single viewport and test the saved arrangement by restoring it as follows.

1 From the View drop-down menu, select Viewports and then 1 Viewport. AutoCAD shows a single display of the current viewport.

2 To return to the LINKAGE-saved arrangement, pick View > Viewports > New Viewports, and then pick the Named Viewports tab. The LINKAGE viewport appears listed. Highlight it and click OK.

The View Command

The View command allows you to save a particular view of a drawing. You may save a view and restore it at a later stage. For example, a saved view can be accessed during the Plot command. Here are the steps to create a view and then restore it:

Saving and restoring a view can speed up work on large complex drawings.

1 Zoom to set a view you want to save.

2 At the command line, type 'view' and press Enter. The View dialog box opens. Pick the Named Views tab.

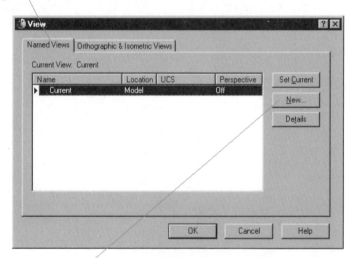

3 Pick on the New button.

Save a view of an area of the drawing you want to plot separately.

4 Enter a name for the view and pick OK and OK again to close all the dialog boxes.

The view has now been saved and can be recalled or used in plotting the drawing. To restore a saved and named view use the menu command sequence: View > Named Views.

The Plotting Procedure

A drawing can be plotted/printed at any scale. You can also ask AutoCAD LT 2000 to 'fit' a drawing on any sheet size, regardless of whether it is an A4 or A0 or larger.

The Plot command is available on the File drop-down menu. You can also type plot at the command line.

The Plot dialog box is quite complex. Only some of the options can be covered in this text. The steps involved in printing a drawing are:

 You can change the electronic paper size even when you have finished a drawing.

1 Select the printer/plotter the drawing will be printed on. If you have several printers/plotters, this is an important step because it can determine the size of the paper you can use. AutoCAD LT does not allow you to plot to a sheet size larger than your printer can print to.

2 Decide the size of the paper to print on.

3 Decide on the scale of the plot. If you set the electronic sheet before you started drawing to a multiple of the standard paper sizes (A1, A2, A3, etc) then this step is easy.

4 Decide whether you want to print to the Drawing Limits/Extents/Display or a Saved View. Limits is out to the size of the electronic paper size; Extents is out to the very edge of the actual drawing; Display is what you can see on the screen before you issue the Plot command; View allows you to select pre-saved views (see the View command).

5 Preview the plot to see that it works OK. This is an essential step. It can save a considerable amount of time and paper.

6 Plot the drawing.

Plotting Work from Model Space

Issue the Print command: File > Print... The Plot dialog box appears.

1 Select the Plot Device tab and pick here to choose your printer.

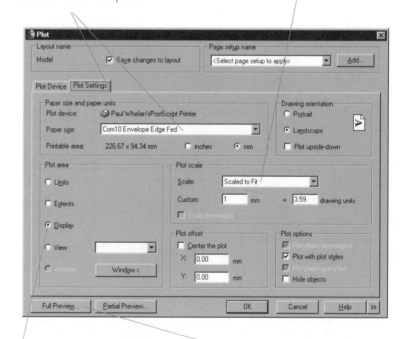

2 Select the Plot Settings tab and choose the sheet size at which to plot.

3 Choose: 'Scaled to Fit' here and AutoCAD LT selects a plot scale for you to fit the drawing on the selected paper size.

4 To print what's on the screen, click Display.

5 Select Full Preview button to see how the plot will appear.

...cont'd

 Check the electronic paper size you set up initially. Use it to work out a plot scale.

6 After viewing the preview, you might decide to rotate the drawing 90 degrees. To do so, select Portrait or Landscape mode, or to turn the drawing 180 degrees, pick: 'Plot upside-down'.

7 Click to Portrait and then try the Full Preview option again.

8 When satisfied with the preview, click on OK in the Print/ Plot Configuration dialog box.

 If you are lost for a scale try plot to 'fit'. See what calculation AutoCAD LT 2000 makes and then round it off.

Printing problems?

Many problems associated with printing are due to either not having a plotter set up correctly or not having the electronic drawing page set up correctly.

These are two areas you should examine carefully if you cannot print drawings at the correct scale. The example given on the facing page, forced the drawing to fit on a sheet of paper. To plot to a specific scale, the scale must be entered in the Plot dialog box.

If you usually work with A3 pages with drawings at 1:100, then it is a good idea to set up your electronic page at 100 times the size of the A3 page. When you need to plot on A3 paper the drawing must be reduced 100 times. This method saves time.

 A plot to fit scale of 283.464 to 25002 can be rounded off to a 1:100 plot scale.

Plotting a Named View

On page 184, a view of a drawing was saved. To plot this view, carry out the following steps.

1 Pick the View button at the bottom left of the Plot dialog box.

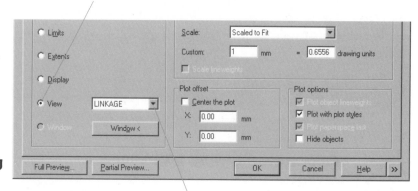

Views can be used to plot selected areas of the drawing at different scales.

2 Click the down-arrow to the right of the View button. Any saved views are available here. Select LINKAGE view.

3 Select the Preview button. The view displays.

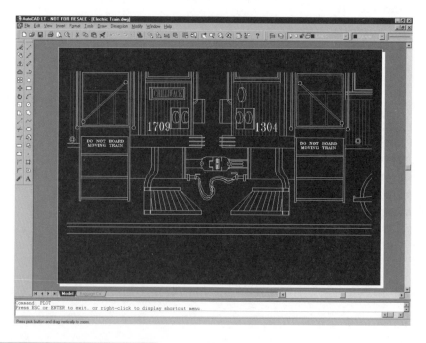

Index